Invest, Work & Live in China

A Comprehensive Legal Guide for Foreign Enterprises

and Expatriates to Invest, Work & Live in China

By

Dr. Dennis Chi-Wing Tang

Ms. Camille Kai-Man Hui

To Asher, Hannah, Alycia, Sunday, Elkan

Good planning and hard work lead to prosperity,

but hasty shortcuts lead to poverty. (Proverbs 21:5)

The content of this book is not intended as, and should not be taken as, legal advice. The use of the information provided in this book should not be taken as establishing any contractual or other form of lawyer-client relationship. Do not act or refrain from acting based upon information provided in this book without first consulting a lawyer about your particular factual and legal circumstances. Due to the limited time on writing this book, mistakes and omissions are inevitable, readers should read the original texts of laws and regulations in all cases. Your feedback for improvement is very much appreciated. For any feedback and enquiry, please contact us at our website www.chinalawservices.com.

CONTENTS

PART I - Welcome to China!

- China at a Glance   8
- Political System   9
- Legal System   10
- Financial System   11
- Economy 12
- Language   15
- Business etiquette   16
- Relationship with Hong Kong   18
- Business Environment for Foreign Investors   20
- Due Diligence   23
- Antitrust and Competition   23
- Business Vehicles   25
- Labor   32
- Accounting and Tax   37
- Intellectual Property   42
- Winding up of a Company   46
- Dispute Resolution   47

PART II - Investing in China

- My business in foreign country is running quite well that we may want to expand into China. Are all kinds of business nature welcomed in China?   51
- A friend recommended me to invest into a Chinese Company for its shares, what are the major areas I should be aware of?   53
- What are the fundamentals for start doing business in China?   55
- What are the risks of doing business without having a proper

- entity? 58
- Why foreign investor should start with Hong Kong before entering into China market? 61
- How shall I choose between WFOE and RO for my business? 63
- How can one transfer money in and out of China? 66
- As an owner of foreign company, shall I be the legal representative of our China subsidiary? 71
- What should be paid attention to when Foreign-invested Enterprise in China hiring Chinese employees? 73
- What are the arrangements for Foreign-invested Enterprises in China to hire expatriates as employees? 75
- Can an employer freely fire an employee during probation period? 80
- I am running a retail business. Can I adopt all the promotion activities and strategies in China as what I did in other countries? 85
- How shall the liability be shared between employer and employee if accidents happen on employees hired by Foreign-invested Enterprise during office hour? 87
- What are the major areas of concerns for Foreign Enterprises to sign cooperation agreements with Chinese entities? 90
- Can Chinese entity and Foreign Enterprise decide the jurisdiction of their contracts? 93
- My foreign company has a sales and purchase agreement with a Chinese entity. We receive the rumors that the Chinese company is to be closed soon when we are about to deliver our goods, what can we do? 96
- There are two different terms about deposits when entering a China-relate contract, which terminology is better and what are their differences? 97
- Products of our company have been counterfeited in China. What can I do? 99

- Since the business is not ideal as expected, I intend to cease the operation of the business in China. What should I do? 102
- I run business in China under my personal capacity, but I failed and ended with debts. Can I apply for bankruptcy? 104

PART III Working & Living in China

- If I frequently represent my company to work in China, do I need any application? 108
- What are the major concerns for expatriate to work in China as employee? 109
- What are the details I should be aware of if I sign employment contract with company in China? 112
- My Chinese colleagues have joined the social security insurance scheme, do I need one too? 115
- How shall I pay tax if I always live in foreign countries but employed in China? 119
- If I work and live frequently in China, am I eligible to apply Chinese Nationality? 122
- I work frequently in Shenzhen with a stable place of residence in China, shall I apply the resident permit? 124
- What are the major areas of concerns if I rent a place of residence in China? 126
- What should I pay attention to if I drive in China? 128
- In case of car accident on the road, what should I do? 131
- How can I claim for compensation if I purchased defective goods or service in China? 135
- I am not a local Chinese. What do I need to pay attention to when I seek medical advice from hospital in China? 140
- As expatriate, am I eligible to get married in China? 141
- I intend to apply divorce with my spouse who is a Chinese, how should I proceed with the application? 143

- Is a divorced wife liable for the debts of her ex-husband? 147
- I intend to purchase real estate property in China. The real estate agents introduced 'small-property-rights housing' to me and says they are cheaper. Can I buy them? 152
- I owned a real estate property in China and intended to rent it out, what are the risks I should be aware of? 154
- The price of real estate property in China goes up and down like roller-coaster ride, what should the buyer do if the seller refuses to complete the transfer procedure when the price goes up? 157
- My dad has just passed away. How should I proceed the application if I want to succeed his deposits in China bank accounts and two apartments? 161
- My assets in China shall only belong to my sons and daughters in the future? 164
- What are the ways to transfer my apartment in China under the name of my kids? 170

PART IV Frequently Asked Questions on Chinese Law

- What happens if I get caught working illegally in China? 172
- When expatriates breaking law in China, will they be treated differently? 174
- My money in my China bank account has been wrongly transferred to the swindler. What should I do? 177
- Is it illegal to play mahjong or cards in China? 180
- What should I do if my pet bites others? 185
- I heard that private lending in China is illegal, isn't it? 187
- Is there a maximum interest rate for lending money to others? 190
- I know that driving after drinking in China is illegal. What is the difference between 'drink driving' and 'drunk driving'? 193
- Arrest for illegal posting on internet is heard from time to time,

- what kind of posting will lead to criminal prosecution? 195
- Is prostitution illegal in China? 197
- If I earn small amount of cash in China, can I bring them along with me when I return to my own country? 198
- What expatriates should pay attention to when they are suspected of criminal offences in China? 201
- When I was suspected of criminal offence, shall I remain silence? 202
- I wish to file a civil litigation in China, what should I pay attention to? 204
- I have already won a final judgment in a foreign court against the defendant who has a property in China. Can I take a judgment of foreign jurisdiction to enforce it in China? 207
- My Chinese Enterprise believes that an administrative action made by the local government is unreasonable and may harm the interests of enterprise. What can I do? 210
- I was served as defendant in a civil case for no reason, can I ignore him? 212
- If an expatriate has not broken the law, why is he prohibited from leaving China? 213

PART I - Welcome to China!

China at a Glance

- Population: 1.4 billion
- Size: 9,597,000 sq. km
- Major cities: Beijing (Capital), Shanghai, Shenzhen, Guangzhou, Hangzhou, Chongqing, Chengdu, Tianjin, Xian
- Currency: Renminbi (RMB / CNY / ¥)
- Languages: Mandarin is widely spoken, many other forms of Chinese dialect are also used, with over a dozen of dialect groups, depending on the classification.
- GDP: Approx. USD10, 000 per capita (2019), nearly 5 times of India
- Unemployment rate: 3.8% (2019)
- Typical office hours: 9:00 – 12:00, 14:00-17:00, Monday to Friday

China (In this book, we refer to Mainland China, a geographical concept that refers to most of the lands in China, excluding Hong Kong, Macau Special Administrative Regions and Taiwan) is the world's second largest economy. China is the world's most populous country in the world, with over a hundred cities. China has its unique business culture. Since the introduction of market reforms in 1978, China's annual GDP growth has a high average of 10%. China is now not only the world's largest exporter, but also the second largest importer. The country maintains an excellent growth rates, despite a modest slowdown in recent years.

Economy is the most important part of China's development, and the government is working hard to move the economy up along the value chain. In coming years, Chinese economy will be dependent less on heavy industry and manufacturing, and services, domestic consumption and technology business will become increasingly important instead. In recent years, China has implemented the Five-year plan and Belt & Road Initiative which pave the way for country-wide development in relation to promotion of sustainable and green growth with long-term and large-scale projects.

China has a growing middle-class consumers which has a high demand of a wide range of consumer goods ranging from smartphones, electronics products, and automobiles to luxury goods. Online retailing is growing at a very rapid rate. According to researchers, over 50% of urban households are classified as middle-class (i.e. household with an annual income between USD 20,000 to USD 40,000).

Political System

The politics of the People's Republic of China (PRC) is a framework of socialist republic run by the Communist Party of China, headed by General Secretary. State power within China is exercised through the Communist Party, the Central People's Government and their provincial and local representation. National People's Congress (NPC) is the primary power of the state, and the country's constitution guaranteed the leading role of the Communist Party in China. Government policy is the critical shaping force of the economy and the society of the country.

Legal System

The China legal system is based primarily on the civil law system. The system is officially referred to as the 'Socialist legal system with Chinese characteristics'. The development of the legal system goes hand-in-hand with the current society's conditions which is described as the early stage of socialism and is in line with development status of the country's economy.

The central government rules the country according to law with a goal to build a socialist country under rules and regulations of the law. All government authorities in China will ensure every aspects of the country including social life to comply with law and will guarantee the full implementation of rule of law throughout different development of the country.

The reform, going-up and modernization of China give rise to internal demand, motivation and practical experience for the construction of a competent legal system. The more intensive the reform opening up and moving forward, the greater extent of development and modernization and the more enormous effect of development of economic society, resulted in a continuous improvement of the Chinese socialist legal system.

The legal traditions and systems in Hong Kong and Macau are different and separated from that of the Mainland China under the 'One country, two systems' constitutional arrangement.

One country, two systems is a principle proposed by Deng Xiaoping who was the paramount reader of PRC for the reunification of China during early 1980s. As of today, the legal systems of Hong Kong and Macau continue to develop based on English Common

Law and Portuguese Civil Law respectively.

Financial System

The China banking system is transforming to a more open system in order to support China's emergence into global economic arena after decades of communism and state ownership. The program started in the early 1980s and it continues until now.

The Chinese banking system used to be centralized with the People's Bank of China as a central bank and sole entity to be authorized to operate in our country. Until early 1980s, the government allowed state-owned specialized banks to accept deposits and conduct banking business. Those specialized banks include the Industrial & Commercial Bank of China, China Construction Bank, Bank of China, Bank of Communications, and Agricultural Bank of China. In 1994, the Chinese government established three more banks, each of which was dedicated to specific lending purpose. These policy-making banks include the Agricultural Development Bank of China, the China Development Bank and the Export-Import Bank of China. The specialized banks are all listed now and owned by the public in various degree, with the majority of shares owned by central government.

China approves the operation of some commercial banks and hundreds of city commercial banks and local banks in rural areas. Foreign banks are also allowed to establish their branches in China for strategic investments in many of the state-owned commercial banks.

As China's economy grows, the government authority had initiated the establishment of Asian Infrastructure Investment Bank in 2015. Over the last decade, China had made significant progress in making Renminbi an international currency. Renminbi is becoming an increasingly important global currency for both trade and investment. There are recently major developments that help the internationalization of Renminbi including the International Monetary Fund's decision to add Renminbi as part of its Special Drawing Rights (SDR) calculation, which is an international reserve asset managed by the organization (The value of the SDR is now based on a basket of five currencies—the U.S. dollar, the Euro, the Chinese Renminbi, the Japanese Yen, and the British Pound). There are also plans that trade and payments along the Belt and Road Initiative will be made in Renminbi, which will further promote the Renminbi's role in international and cross-border payments.

China's Renminbi is backed by the world's largest foreign exchange reserves, totaling more than 3 trillion US Dollars. After all, China is the largest foreign country creditor of U.S. (the U.S. debt to China is USD 1.11 trillion as of May 2019), and Japan comes second.

Foreign investors can enjoy a wide range of channels to invest into China's financial market as the country has an ongoing plan to internationalize its currency and open up its capital markets.

Economy

China is the world's second largest economy by nominal GDP and is one of the world's fastest-growing major countries, with an average growth rates of near 10% over last 30 years, and the growth is between 6-7% in recent years. According to the IMF, based on a per capita income basis, China ranked 67th by GDP (nominal) and 73rd by GDP (PPP) per capita in 2018. China has an estimated RMB23 trillion worth of natural resources, 90% of which are coal and rare earth metals. China has the world's largest total banking sector assets of RMB39.93 trillion (RMB 268.76 trillion) with RMB27.39 trillion in total deposits.

The Chinese government aims to achieve a 'moderately well-off' society 2021 and to become a well-developed nation through modernization by 2049. 2049 is the 100th anniversary of establishment of the government of the People's Republic of China.

Our country is promoting innovation and pushing forward high-quality development. China ranked 28th in the Global Competitiveness Report 2018 by the World Economic Forum. China's innovation score (64.4) is close to Italy's (65.8), not too far from Australia's (69.8), and ranked much higher than countries like India (53.8) and Russia (50.7).

China's huge manufacturing business makes it the world's largest exporter, supplying the world everything from soft toys to smartphones. The improving global economy of western countries support the continuous growth of China's manufacturing business. At the same time, China is the world's second largest importer. Natural resources account for a large portion of the country's purchases and increasing portion of consumer goods. Domestic consumption plays an increasingly important role, as the country shifts away from an investment and export-led growth model.

China's fast growing and enormous market size cannot be overlooked as an investment destination. The economy is evolving to a domestic consumption driven model since Chinese people are willing to spend more on goods and services.

Being the world's fastest-growing consumer market and second-largest importer of goods, China is a net importer of services products. China is the largest trading nation in the world and plays an important role in international trade and has increasingly engaged in trade organizations and treaties in recent years. China became a member of the World Trade Organization in 2001. It also signed free trade agreements with many nations and international organizations, including ASEAN, Australia, New Zealand, Pakistan, South Korea and Switzerland. Under the 'One Country, Two systems' framework, Mainland China signed a series of free trade agreements with Hong Kong (and Macau) known as Mainland and Hong Kong Closer Economic Partnership Arrangement (CEPA). CEPA covers four areas: trade in goods, trade in services, investment, economic and technical cooperation. Investors shall note the provinces in the coastal regions of China tend to be more industrialized while regions in the hinterland (inner region), such as western areas of the country, are less developed.

China's Belt and Road Initiative is expected to further support future economic growth as it improves our connectivity with more than 60 countries in Asia, the Middle East, Africa and Europe. The Belt and Road Initiative was introduced by President Xi in 2013 to promote co-operation among 65 countries in Asia, Europe and Africa along the ancient land based 'silk road economic belt' and the '21st maritime silk road'. The main areas of Belt and Road co-operation include policy coordination, infrastructure connectivity, trade and investment, financial integration and cultural exchange.

Many countries in Asia have deepening economic ties with China. For instance, Singapore, Malaysia and other countries from South-East Asia, are all look to China as their major trade partner. Growth across the region is being fuelled by China's expanding economic importance. Purchasing activities include importing electronic components and equipment from South-East Asia countries like Thailand and Singapore, as well as buying raw commodities such as rice, palm oil, rubber and coal from places including Malaysia and Indonesia. In addition, China's outbound tourism market is buoying hotels, resorts, tourist attractions and shopping malls around Asia. Not surprisingly, property investments are one of major targets for China's outbound funds.

China invests heavily in Asian infrastructure with large projects, in particular along the Belt and Road areas. More than 60 countries have now partnered with China to create commercial links that track ancient trade routes to enhance the trading and infrastructure network that reaches out from China's borders.

Language

Learning Chinese language can be a challenge. Yet the challenge is worth your effort as doing business in China is certainly rewarding.

Chinese characters and words are difficult to learn, in particular written Chinese. Words under the English Language system are created out of alphabets A-Z with vowels, consonants and origins of meaning for each word, while the Chinese language system is composed of logograms to develop its characters. In order to understand the content of a newspaper, the reader should know at least 3,000 Chinese characters. A well-educated Chinese shall know more than 3,000 Chinese characters.

Mandarin (also known as Putonghua) is the only official spoken language in China. Mandarin consisted of intonations is a language difficult to learn. Different tones used when speaking Mandarin can determine its meaning. Learning different languages require persistency and proactiveness. Expatriates (called 'Laowai'in Mandarin) speaking fluent Mandarin as second language are increasing which means foreigners learning Mandarin is achievable over time.

The population of English speakers will mostly cluster in downtown areas of major cities in China. Therefore, it is helpful for foreigners to learn a few simple phrases in Mandarin. For getting around, please note that English is not an official language in China, therefore it is not widely used at work or within the government operation.

Apart from Mandarin, there are different dialects widely spoken in China such as Cantonese in Guangdong Province, Shanghainese in Shanghai, Min in Fujian. There are also other ethnic minorities in China speaking their own languages.

Business etiquette

If I have to pick a single important Chinese business etiquette and explain to my expatriate friends, that will be *Guanxi* (which means 'Relationship'). Guanxi has a major influence in running businesses in China, and it carries a much more complex meaning than just relationship or connections. It also includes interpersonal links and reciprocal obligations that come from one's social network. In China, developing a strong network of trusted partners will be very helpful, especially when it comes to introductions and negotiations. Guanxi is believed to be an important factor when it comes to being successful in China. Guanxi is developed in scenarios like growing up or working together, helping each other, networking or participating in social activities aimed at strengthening the relationship and personal trust.

Another important business etiquette concept is 'Mianzi' (which means 'Face'). Mianzi is an important concept one should understand when living and working in China. Mianzi is a combination of social standing, influence, dignity and honour. Mianzi or Face is something related to honour. For example, saving face (means honour), losing face (means disgrace) or giving face (means respect) are crucial elements in business life. No Chinese wants to be embarrassed or made to feel insignificant or laughed at in the office or business activities. Respect for people's feelings is crucial. Every person's reputation, dignity and prestige counts. Mianzi is not only applied to individual, but also companies and entities. We give somebody face by flattering them or showing respect. Act patronizingly to others may mean losing face to them. Certainly, humiliating people in the public or even via personal email also means losing face to the one.

The concept of Mianzi is a critical part of many interactions among people including business partners, friends and family members. This concept is also reflected in hierarchy and reputation regime in China. Hierarchy or ranking counts, whether it is about a seating position in the boardroom or at the banqueting table, or who speaks first in a meeting.

We will suggest our expatriate friends to be punctual, shake hands and be prepared to give out business cards in the first meeting. Nodding is also a common greeting. Of course, one will be judged further on whether his attitude is suitably respectful, from gift-giving, entertaining, and asking about family members and recent personal life. Promoting harmony with business partners and friends is always a good practice.

Relationship with Hong Kong

As part of China, Hong Kong (The Hong Kong Special Administrative Region) is in proximity to Mainland China. With a special relationship with the central government, Hong Kong is an important gateway for conducting business in Mainland China. Hong Kong has intensive and extensive business influence across Mainland China and contributes a significant part of the Mainland inbound investment. Hong Kong and Mainland China are each other's major trading partner.

Per the speech of Premier Li in 2019, central government rated high importance to investments from Hong Kong (and Macau) because they accounted for nearly 70 per cent of all the total foreign investments in the Mainland China. According to Hong Kong government statistics, Hong Kong is the Mainland's largest source of realized foreign direct investment, accounting for about 54.0% of the national total as of end-2018, with cumulative value reaching HKD8,616.6 billion (USD 1,099.2 billion). At the same time, Mainland is Hong Kong's second largest source of inward direct investment. At end-2017, investment from the Mainland accounted for about 25.5% or HKD 3,872.4 billion (USD 496.8 billion) of the total stock of Hong Kong's inward direct investment.

The co-operation and integration between Hong Kong and the Mainland China provided great business opportunities to foreign investors. One example is the Closer Economic Partnership

Arrangement (CEPA), the main text of which was signed in June 2003 and keep strengthening and updating every year. CEPA was the first free trade agreement ever entered into by the central government (PRC, Mainland China) and Hong Kong. It opened up huge opportunities for Hong Kong businesses, allowing Hong Kong goods and services to gain greater access to the Mainland China market. CEPA is also beneficial to the Mainland China because Hong Kong as a 'super-connector' for Mainland China enterprises to reach the global market and facilitating China's integration with the global economy. Foreign investors can also establish businesses in Hong Kong to leverage the CEPA benefits with its renowned stable legal system and low tax environment, at the same time tapping into the vast opportunities with Mainland China market.

According to the Global Financial Centers Index report 2019, Hong Kong has been ranked among the top 3 global financial hubs, following New York and London. Hong Kong is also the pioneer in offshore Renminbi (RMB) businesses. Hong Kong was the first offshore market to launch RMB businesses in 2004. The market for RMB businesses is fast growing and various offshore RMB products and services have been launched in Hong Kong to cope with the business demands of both local and foreign enterprises and financial institutions. The positive development of the offshore RMB market will surely generate more business opportunities for investors and market participants in Hong Kong, and further strengthen Hong Kong's position as Asia's leading financial center and an important gateway for the China market.

Business Environment for Foreign Investors

In the World Bank's Ease of Doing Business Index published in May 2018, China ranked 46 (and Hong Kong ranked No.4) which is well over the regional average. In addition to that, China ranked very high, No.6 on the enforcement of contracts.

The Chinese government kept on its effort in facilitating doing business in China by simplifying the registration process such as minimize the basic routine procedures in obtaining business license, organization certification and tax registration. The local tax authorities have eased the process for corporations to file tax assessment and pay taxes.

Please take note that the Catalogue for the Guidance of Foreign Investment Industries is an important document for foreign investors investing in China. It clearly stated the three different categories of industry sectors for overseas corporations to invest in, namely 'encouraged', 'restricted' or 'prohibited'.

Foreign investment in the 'encouraged' industries may enjoy preferential terms from local authorities. .In the Special Economic Zone or new Free Trade Zones of the country, a shorter 'Negative list' ('banned list') may be used to lay out only the restricted industries. Any types of foreign-invested business out of the negative list('banned list') are allowed and will enjoy equal treatment similar to that of domestic one.

The following reasons further illustrated why foreign investors are attracted to invest into China:

- China is one of the most important trading countries, be it in terms of buying or selling. It is the world's largest exporter and the

second largest importer of merchandise. Obvious enough, with a population of 1.4 billion, China itself is tremendous buyers' market.
- China is one of the world's largest digital or technological economies. Refer to the recent popular talks about HUAWEI and the development of 5G industry, China is now in a very advanced position in many areas of technology. Taken the mobile payment gateway as example, the total spending amount via mobile payment platform in 2016 is USD 5.5. trillion, an amount which is 50 times more than the US. Researches had shown that over 60 per cent of global mobile payment users are from China in 2018.
- Low labor costs. Despite the recent increase in wages, China is still offering a relatively low-cost labor force, especially in the remote rural areas of the country.
- The spending power of middle-class and local Chinese in China is expeditious. The rise of 400 million of young middle-class is influenced by the high annual GDP growth. Apart from the increasing spending power, a growing interest for luxurious brands and imported products can also be observed.
- China is in the stage of transition from high-speed to high-quality growth, from exports to local consumption, from heavy industry to services and high- technology, for the government has planned to add value and become a high-income country by 2030.
- Chinese laws in relation to foreign investments have been largely relaxed in recent years. China's new Foreign Investment Law (FIL) may reshape how foreign investment is regulated in China. The National People's Congress just passed this new law on March 15, 2019 and it will be officially taken into effect on January 1, 2020. The goal of the 2019 FIL is to create a more stable, transparent, and predictable environment for foreign investment in China by fundamentally changing how foreign-invested enterprises (FIE) are regulated. The new law also calls for the setup of a comprehensive 'investment service system' which aims to assist foreign entities that invest in China by providing information about laws, regulations,

policies, and investment project information. Though the FIL is incomplete, it is a good move in the right direction to many foreign business organizations. The FIL covers almost a full spectrum of foreign investment and applies to both natural persons and corporate entities from foreign countries regarding the following business activities:

- Establish foreign-invested enterprises in China;
- Invest in new projects;
- Acquire shares of stock, equity interests, property rights, or other similar rights or interests involving local Chinese enterprises; and
- Invest in China through other means.

- The local authorities continue to provide benefits to foreign investment in encouraged sectors. In general, the benefits include tax recession and preferential tax policies such as tax holidays or exemptions offered to foreign investors which means foreign investors can participate in a wider scope of business and enjoy lower cost at the same time. For instance, investors investing into integrated circuit products can enjoy tax holidays up to 5 years. (An integrated circuit or monolithic integrated circuit (also referred to as an IC, a chip, or a microchip) is a set of electronic circuits on one small flat piece (or 'chip') of semiconductor material that is normally silicon.) In less developed region in China such as the western part of Xinjiang province, further incentives for investment may be granted to investors. For benefits for new High Technologies, those companies, may enjoy both a 15% p.a. reduced rate of tax and eligible to an additional 50% deduction for R&D expenses. Other benefits may also be available, including value added tax, customs and income tax deduction, or direct subsidize to qualified professional, to foreign investment in a Special Economic Zone, Free Trade Zone or in special sectors and areas. Special terms and rate for land use maybe available in 2nd and 3rd-tier cities to attract foreign investors.

Due Diligence

China ranked No.6 on the enforcement of contracts according to the World Bank's Ease of Doing Business Index published 2018, the high position of China worth your attention. We always remind our clients to spend effort on documents and implement a comprehensive record and filing system in order to protect their interest when investing into China. Therefore, when our clients are planning to invest into a China business or cooperating with any Chinse entities, they are advised to conduct thorough legal due diligence.

Due diligence is an investigation that a reasonable company or person is expected to take before entering into an agreement or contract with another party. A common example of due diligence is potential investor investigates a target company or its assets before an acquisition. Due diligence provides investor a clearer picture on validity, costs, benefits, and potential risks of the activities. As lawyers, we always remind our clients that it is wiser for them to spend less at the beginning stage for legal due diligence rather than risking themselves into costly litigation when disputes arise later on.

Antitrust and Competition

China's first comprehensive competition law, The Anti-Monopoly

Law (2008), prohibits monopolistic conduct, and is divided into the following three major areas:

- Anti-competitive agreements between undertakings;
- Abuse of a dominant position;
- Mergers that may have the effect of eliminating or restricting competition.

There are other relevant legislations such as, the Anti-Unfair Competition Law, Bidding Law, Price Law, Contract Law and Foreign Trade Law, and the recently implemented Foreign Investment Law.

Under the Anti-Monopoly Law, the State Council established two regulatory bodies to regulate monopolistic activity:

- The Anti-Monopoly Committee is responsible for developing competition legislation and policy, publishing guidelines and coordinating the administrative enforcement work.
- The Anti-Monopoly Enforcement Agency is responsible for enforcing the Anti-Monopoly Law.

Under the Anti-Monopoly Law, individuals and companies are entitled to bring private actions against undertakings that have engaged in monopolistic conduct. The Anti-Monopoly Law prohibits 'monopoly agreements' which includes agreements, decisions or other concerted practices between business operators that have the purpose or effect of eliminating or restricting competition. A classical precedent case of Antitrust law in China is the disapproval of the Chinese authorities against a USD 2.4 billion acquisition of famous beverage giant, Huiyuan Juice by Coca-Cola in 2009.

Business Vehicles

When foreign investors plan to enter the China market, they should first consider whether they would like to setup a legal entity with capital investment or they would just test the water by working with local agents and representatives.

Individual Industrial and Commercial Households (for local small family business), limited companies, partnerships and sometimes the variable interest entity ('VIE') arrangement for foreign-related investment are the main forms of business vehicle in China.

A VIE is operation controlled by contractual arrangements instead of majority voting rights by shareholders. VIE has a unique position in China. Take Alibaba as example, as the world's largest retailer and e-commerce company, Alibaba uses a VIE structure allowing U.S. citizens to purchase VIE shares in Alibaba in New York Stock Exchange (NYSE). This implies that foreign investor can use VIE for foreign investment in China in a wider scope of business or industries such as the internet business and education sector.

VIEs are important issue in China because they can enable a foreign Investor to invest in a sector that would otherwise be prohibited to foreign investment, such as the internet or education sector.)

Wholly Foreign-Owned Enterprise

The Wholly Foreign-Owned Enterprise (WFOE) is a limited liability company wholly owned by the foreign investor(s) and it is one of the most popular types of foreign-invested entities for doing business in China. Any enterprise in China which is 100% owned by a foreign company or companies can be called as WFOE. The registered capital of a WFOE shall be contributed solely by foreign investor(s) and is shall not include branches established in China by foreign enterprises and/or any other foreign economic organizations. However, according to Chinese law, the definition of 'branches of the WFOE' is not absolutely clear in which 'branches' shall include both the branch companies engaged in operational activities and representative offices, which are generally not engaged in direct business activities. Therefore, branches and representative offices set up by foreign enterprises are not WFOE. WFOE has great potential in China, setting up a WFOE can facilitate investors to:

- conduct business activities and generate revenue within the defined scope of business, and
- hire local and foreign employees directly.

It usually takes two to six months to set up a WFOE, depending on the nature of business, scope of services and its location. Please note that the concept of 'virtual office ' is generally not accepted by the local authorities and banks.

In China, WFOEs were originally conceived for encouraged manufacturing activities that were either export orientated or introduced advanced technology. However, after China's entry into the WTO, these conditions were gradually abolished and the WFOE is increasingly being used for service providers such as a variety of consulting and management services, software development and trading as well. With that, any enterprise in China which is 100% owned by a foreign company or companies can be called as WFOE.

In 2014, China amended its Company Law to abolish minimum capital requirements. However, many cities in China still impose its own capital requirements for setting up a company, especially for foreign invested companies. If any business is subjected to additional licensing requirements, then a minimum capital requirement may be imposed. The amount of minimum capital depends on the location and the nature of the business. It is either written in the rules or the local government authorities will review the application to determine whether the amount one intended to invest is sufficient for the business activity. A company's registered capital may have implication to more than just registration, such as:

- Support from government. Obviously local government tends to provide more support and favorable terms for larger scale of foreign investment. The register capital will also affect a company's general VAT taxpayer status (tax rate) and export VAT rebate applications.
- Acquiring new business or setting up branch office. The ability to make future changes to a company's structure, setting up branch office, acquiring new business and change in scope of business could be hindered by a low registered capital.
- The application of local employees' residence permits. With a low registered capital, companies may not be able to sponsor temporary residence permits or permanent change of residential addresses for local employees who reside outside the administrative district where the company is located. This could sometimes forcibly limit a company's talent pool. In similar way, recruitment of foreign employees may also be affected, as some local authorities impose rules on the number of foreign employees that a company can employ based on that company's registered capital.

The shareholder of a WFOE can either be a natural person (foreigner) or a foreign company. Whenever possible, we always suggest our client to use a foreign company (in particular a Hong

Kong limited company) as shareholder of a WFOE for many reasons, including the case of transfer of share at lower tax rate for foreign corporate entity vs to individual which is 10% and 20% respectively.

Basic Step of Setting up a WFOE in consulting industry

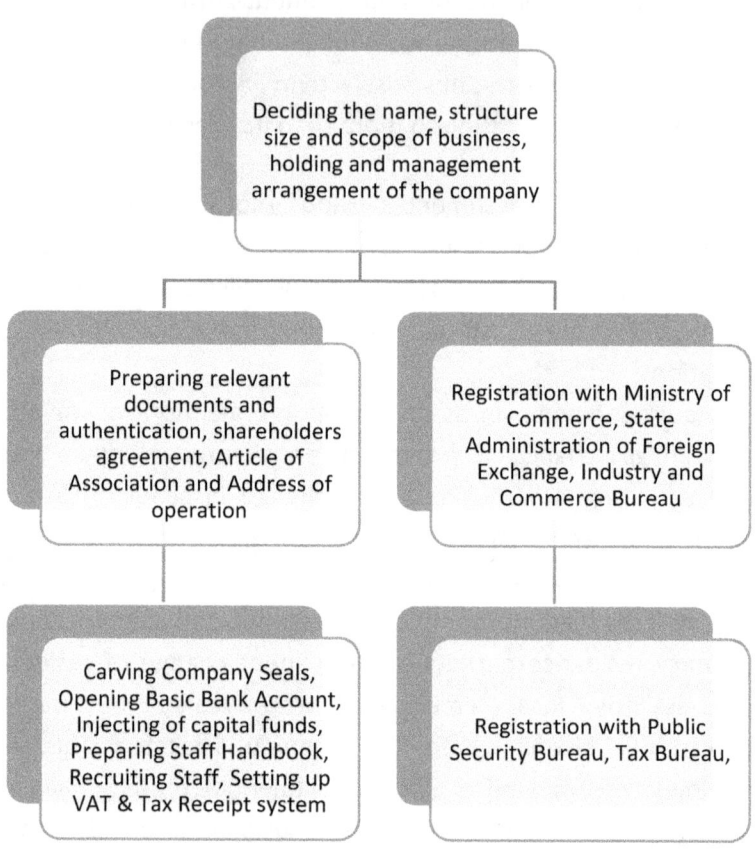

Joint Ventures

There are two major form of joint venture (JV) structure in the China market:

- The Equity Joint Venture (EJV) requires capital investments from both local and foreign entities. The percentage of the capital investment determines the amount of profit and risk that both the foreign and local company is responsible for. Foreign investors entering business sectors where WFOEs are prohibited may use the format of Equity Joint Venture, although this is less prevalent nowadays as more sectors are being opened up to WFOEs. The share percentage hold by foreign investor of an EJV shall not be less than 25% in general, and if so, the EJV cannot enjoy favorable terms designated for foreign-invested EJV.
- The Cooperative Joint Venture (CJV) is another type of partnership in which the Chinese and foreign parties cooperate on the basis of a joint venture contract. The risk and amount of profit shared by each party is not determined by the capital investment, rather it is agreed beforehand at the beginning of the cooperation. CJV were more frequently used in the 1990s when the local companies in China was at the early stage of development. The Law of the People's Republic of China on Chinese-Foreign Cooperative Joint Ventures (the 'Cooperative Joint Venture Law'), promulgated in 1988 and amended on October 31, 2000, essentially confirmed the established practice. 'Contractual joint venture' is another term for cooperative joint venture. International companies often injected funds and technology, while local Chinese companies provided land, equipment and other necessities under CJV. Laws and regulations for establishment of Cooperate JV can vary substantially between sectors. Under the CJV arrangement, the foreign party normally has a priority on collecting back the investment when the CJV has a return in operation. Before entering into a JV relation, be it EJV or CJV, foreign investors shall ensure a clear understanding of the business objectives has been established and exit arrangements have been developed.

Steps that a foreign investor shall take to assess the viability of the

JV are:

- Perform a due diligence on the proposed JV partner for potential legal, financial and reputational issues.
- Prepare a comprehensive JV agreement. As a reminder, disputes arise from a JV agreement must be handled in China and according to Chinese law. Foreign investors often perceived that litigation or arbitration is best done outside China, and preferably in their home country. However, this arrangement is not allowed by Chinese law and in fact provides limited protection to foreign investors.
- Secure a majority of board seats for voting rights and retain the power to appoint the legal representative and the general manager of the JV, this will give foreign investor more effective control over the operation.
- Hire a legal counsel during setting up of the JV and do not rely only on the local partner to undertake the legal and administrative work for establishment, because the interests of both party in this process are not aligned or even conflicting. It is a good idea to retain an independent and experienced China lawyer who also understands the common law system to represent the foreign investor.
- Hire an independent accountant, in addition to the one carrying out the work referred by the local partner. This is to ensure that the foreign investor has a clear and transparency picture on what is happening within the JV.
- Design a good controlling and administration system of important document, such as company certificates, seals, and the bank account operation to ensure that no contracts can be signed, and no money will be paid without foreign investor representative's consent or approval according to due procedure.

Representative Office

Representative Office (RO) represents the interests of a foreign investor by acting as a liaison office for its parent company. There are restrictions on the operations of a RO, and it is getting less popular due to the simplified requirement of a WFOE operation. A RO can conduct market research and develop partnerships and business channels, but all business transactions must be carried out by the parent company, which must be a foreign company. If a foreign investor begins to sell products or services in China, one will require to establish a local company such as WFOE.

A RO is taxed on its expenses as it cannot generate revenues. There are other limitations for running a RO, including the fact that a RO may not hire local employees directly and must rely on a licensed employment agency, and has limited seat for foreign employees.

The good news is, there is no investment requirement because RO is not classified as an independent legal entity in China. Therefore, a RO may be suitable for businesses looking to establish a short-term presence in China without the need to generate revenue.

We should note that RO shall not be regarded simply as a way for new entrants to China to minimize a foreign investor's exposure in the event of failure because RO itself is not an independent entity. RO is just an extension of its parent company and therefore the parent company will then take up all responsibility and liability for its operations in China. In this sense, a WFOE provides greater protection because it is a form of limited liability company isolated from its investors.

Labor

Workforce

Low labor cost was once considered the main factor behind the China economic miracle, however, the rapid economic growth over the past three decades has at the same time led to a continuous increase in wages.

Although majority area of China is still the world's manufacturing hub, and still focusing on labor-intensive, export-driven production of keenly priced goods. But the wages are rising and the growing middle class is expecting for more. The government is leading the society in shifting its focus on producing more value-added goods and services.

The government is keen to avoid the middle-income trap, with a new focus on innovation, higher-end consumption and services. Growth in the service sector, revitalization of industry and the move to more advance innovation now present a bigger opportunity for both local and foreign companies. China has an extremely active private sector and major cities is ripe for a fresh productivity revolution, government initiatives with value-added industries further supporting this change. In addition, the China's fast-growing middle class represents many market opportunities for overseas businesses across a wide range of sectors of the economy. Wages are rising, so as purchasing power.

Labor Law

The labor laws in China are comprehensive and relatively inclined towards the protection of employee's rights. This is not to imply that employers have no power over decisions regarding their employees, but rather companies need to follow more rules during execution of labor contracts to ensure that employees are treated fairly.

A labor contract is mandatory, and it should be finalized no later than the end of the employee's first working month. Otherwise the employer will have to pay double salary up to the period when a formal contract is formed with the employee. If the employee has complete service for a year without signing a valid contract, an open-ended labor contract will be implied automatically between the employer and the employee in which a double pay of the wages shall be applied without an end day.

We will advise clients to have a staff handbook containing company policies and procedures in place at the very beginning of the employment. The handbook shall describe policies specific to the company such as expected working hours, employee benefits and responsibilities, administrative procedures and other details which may not be stated in the employee contact but must be clarified to the employees. The handbook shall be endorsed by labor union (or representative elected) and employees should sign to confirm that they have read through it. Other special working arrangements should first be filed and consented with the labor bureau.

If a company decides to revise certain rules relating to the terms of employment, discussions should be held with both the employee and the labor union or labor representative elected before confirming the decision to revise.

A probation period is generally included in a labor contract if the employee works full-time for a contract of term over three months. The duration of probation is restricted depending on scenarios, and in all cases, probation period shall not exceed 6 months.

The termination of a labor contract may occur at any time by negotiation and consensus between the company and employee or according to due procedure, where the company is liable to pay a severance compensation based on the number of years of service of the employee in most of the situations.

Only in certain scenarios, the company may terminate a labor contract immediately without compensation to the employee, such as if the employee is on probation and fails to measure up to the standards given, then the employer may terminate the employee. That is:

- If the employee commits a serious breach of policy, such as find guilty of dereliction of their duties, or
- the employee holds another employment relationship that affects their duties, the employer also has the right to terminate, or
- a labor contract can be terminated if the employee is convicted to a criminal offense.

On the other side, there are several circumstances where a company must not terminate a labor contract, such as:

- if the employee is on a statutory medical treatment period, or has lost capacity to work due to a work-related injury, then the employer cannot lay off the employee, or
- during a female employee pregnancy or nursing baby (up to the 1 year old) period, the company cannot terminate the contract unless paying full compensation for the full period, or
- If an employee has been working for a company for over fifteen years and is within five years towards retirement age, then again, the employer cannot terminate a labor contract.

If an employer unlawfully terminates a labor contract, the court will instruct the company to reinstate the employee's job if the employee requests so. If the employee does not request to reinstate or it is not possible for them to reinstate, then the employer will have to pay employee the corresponding compensation in full.

A few basic steps are required for a lawful termination of an employee. The first is to collect evidence that can be used to further support employer the claim for justifiable termination of the labor contract. After the evidence has been collected, company should meet with the employee to present the findings. The employer shall communicate with the employee to determine the employee's position in the company and the calculation of unpaid salary and final compensation. Noted that the termination process is only complete upon the signature of a termination agreement by both parties.

If the company are conducting a mass termination under a redundancy situation (greater than twenty people or 10% of the company's total labor force) then the employee needs to pre-file and inform the local labor bureau regarding the redundancy.

Employees are entitled to compensation for overtime pay. If employees work overtime on a regular weekday schedule, each hour of overtime will be compensated at 1.5 times that of the employee's basic pay. If the employees work on a weekend or holiday, overtime payment will increase to 2 times of the basic pay, and in case of overtime work during public holiday such as Chinese New Year, then overtime will be 3 times of the basic pay. Overtime compensation arrangement may not apply to senior management.

The severance compensation of an employee is calculated based upon the number of years one had worked for the company, in general, one-month salary for each year of service with maximum payment of twelve months, and the figure (salary) is based on the City Average Salary and should be capped at 300% of that average. It should also be noted that the salary includes all forms of income, such as annual bonus, travel subsidies, meal allowance etc.

Some employers may want to include a non-competition clause in labor contract as obligation impose on the employee after termination the contract. This arrangement generally applies to senior management, technical staff or other personnel with confidentiality obligations who may then work for a competitor providing similar services or producing similar products. The non-competition clause shall have a maximum period of no longer than two years and the company must pay employee during this period.

Foreign Employer and Employee

A Representative Office in China cannot directly employ staff, and it can only recruit and signing labor contract through a local labor service agency who will hire employees for the representative office on the company's behalf. Expatriates can be employed as representatives of a Representative Office with limited quota.

Foreign-invested enterprises such as WFOE are China limited companies and can hire employees directly. The arrangement of expatriates working in WFOE are similar to working with other local companies who will require to obtain proper work visas and permits ahead.

Accounting and Tax

Accounting

China's accounting standards are similar to that of International Financial Reporting Standards (IFRS). When preparing annual financial reports, all companies shall follow the Chinese Generally Accepted Accounting Principles (Chinese GAAP) which is also known as Chinese Accounting Standards. There are certain differences between the IFRS and Chinese GAAP, for example, reporting must be in RMB but not foreign currencies and all financial reporting must be in Chinese and not in English. The accounting or fiscal year runs from 1st January to 31st December.

A local Chinese accountant will likely prioritize the management of China's Value-Added Tax (VAT) and fapiao system in their daily work. (The VAT fapiao is a physical tax receipt that can be used as a credit against outstanding VAT liabilities. Since these fapiaos effectively serve as a form of tax coupon, or cash, that local accounting practices are heavily inclined towards prioritizing the issuing and receiving of VAT fapiao and, in general to administering the VAT and fapiao system instead of the theoretical accounting standards.) As a result, given that all the China companies including WFOE and JV are required to prepare financial reports at the end of each year based on Chinese GAAP, local accountant may need to make adjusting entries during the annual audit for annual compliance purpose.

In addition, when one is operating a RO or a WFOE in China, one must have his audits and accounts files located in his China office ready for the random inspections by government authorities and processing of annual audit.

Taxes

China is a relatively high tax jurisdiction, and China's tax code is complicated that requires tax report filings in Chinese and in Renminbi, and failure to comply with Chinese tax legislation can lead to substantial penalties. Nevertheless, China has also signed over a hundred of bilateral or multilateral tax agreements to eliminate double taxation and allowing for reduced rates of withholding tax on dividends, royalties and interest. Both central government and local authorities are making efforts to offer tax incentives to foreign investment to stimulate growth. So, do I have to pay tax in China? (Below is a general table, as we expect policy variations exist among cities. Expatriates shall also refer to Double Taxation Agreement, and special arrangement for people from Hong Kong and Macau. Most important of all, please noted that China has just brought a reform of the Individual Income Tax (IIT) regime into force on 1 January 2019)

For regular Employees		Inside China (China-sourced income)		Outside China (non China-sourced Income)	
Days	Status	Borne by Chinese Entity	Borne by Overseas Entity	Borne by Chinese Entity	Borne by Overseas Entity
Less than 183 days	Non-	Yes	Yes or No	No	No
183 days - 1 year	Non-	Yes	Yes	Yes or No	Yes or No
1 year – 5 years	Resident	Yes	Yes	Yes	Yes or No
More than 5 years	Resident	Yes	Yes	Yes	Yes

For Directors and Managerial Personnel		Inside China (China-sourced income)		Outside China (non China-sourced Income)	
Days	Status	Borne by Chinese Entity	Borne by Overseas Entity	Borne by Chinese Entity	Borne by Overseas Entity
Less than 183 days	Non-	Yes	Yes	No	No
183 days - 1 year	Non-	Yes	Yes	Yes	Yes or No
1 year – 5 years	Resident	Yes	Yes	Yes	Yes or No
More than 5 years	Resident	Yes	Yes	Yes	Yes

If you and your company are tax resident of China, I will suggest you seek advice from professionals and help liaising with local authorities directly. The major types of tax in China include:

- Turnover taxes. This comprises three types of taxes, namely, Value-Added Tax (VAT), Consumption Tax and Business Tax (Business Tax is in the process of changing to VAT). The levy of these taxes is normally based on the volume of turnover or sales of the corporations in the manufacturing, circulation or service sectors. Value-added taxes ranged from between 3% and 13%. For example, providing consulting services are subject to 6% VAT, and the sales and importation of goods is 13% VAT, while the rate for small-scale taxpayers can be as low as 3%. A consumption tax is levied on 14 types of luxury and environmentally unfriendly products including alcohol, cigarettes, petroleum, vehicles and jewelry. Business tax is levied on the provision of services, property taxes, land appreciation taxes and customs duties, it varies greatly from 1% to 56%.

VAT Tax Relieve Policy (for a WFOE) in consulting industry

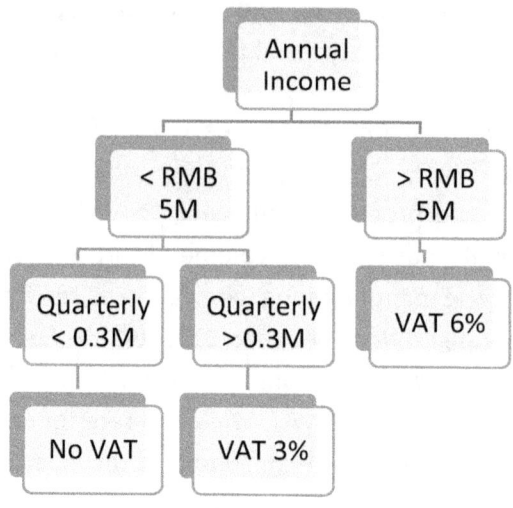

- Income taxes. Income tax levies on the basis of the profits gained by corporations, or the income earned by individuals. China impose a relatively high standard corporate profit tax of 25%, a relatively high tax rate. However, corporate taxes can be lowered with reductions, exemptions and tax holidays if income is derived from certain encouraged sectors of the economy including agriculture, forestry, infrastructure and high-end technology. Noted that foreign-invested enterprises (FIE) are considered a tax resident under China's tax law and are therefore subject to tax on their worldwide off-shore income, while non-resident foreign enterprises will pay 10% on their China-derived income. Under special policies in defined sector or region, the basic standard income tax can be lowered to 15%.
- Individual Income Tax. If an individual is domiciled in China (generally speaking, one spends more than half of his time in Mainland China each year) then he may need to pay China tax on

his worldwide income. The rate is a progressive one starting from 3 up to 45%. Income tax is normally withheld from wages by employers and paid tax on a monthly basis. If an individual is not domiciled but reside in China, he will have to pay tax only on his China-sourced income. However, this theoretically applies only for the first five years. After that tax is still levied on his worldwide income.

Standard Individual Income Tax Rate:

RMB 1,500 or less per month - 3%
RMB 1,500 – 4,500 - 10%
RMB 4500 – 9,000 - 20%
RMB 9,000 – 35,000 - 25%
RMB 35,000 – 55,000 - 30%
RMB 55,000 – 80,000 - 35%
Above RMB 80,000 per month - 45%

- Withholding taxes for Foreign Enterprises. There is a withholding tax of 10% applies to overseas enterprise that do not have establishment or business address in China. This applies to China-sourced income derived from dividends, interest, royalties and property leases, as well as other sources of passive income. I suggest one to check the tax arrangement between China and his home country. The tax treaty may reduce the amount of withholding tax that needs to be paid. Complete set of documents and approval is needed for getting money out of China.
- Customs duties. Customs duties are imposed on the goods and articles imported into and exported out of the territory of China, including Excise Tax.
- Resource taxes. These taxes include Resource Tax and Urban and Township Land Use Tax. These taxes are applicable to the exploiters engaged in natural resource exploitation or to the users

of urban and township land. These taxes reflect the chargeable use of state-owned natural resources and aim to adjust the different profits derived by taxpayers who have access to different availability of natural resources.

- Property taxes. This includes Urban Real Estate Tax and House Property Tax.
- Behavioural taxes. These include Deed Tax, Stamp Tax, Vehicle and Vessel Usage Tax, Vehicle and Vessel Usage License Plate Tax etc. These taxes are levied on specified behaviour.
- Taxes for special purposes. These taxes include City Maintenance and Construction Tax, Farmland Occupation Tax, Fixed Asset Investment Orientation Regulation Tax, Land Appreciation Tax, Vehicle Acquisition Tax etc. These taxes are levied on specific items for special regulative purposes.
- Agricultural taxes. Taxes belonging to this category are Agriculture Tax and Animal Husbandry Tax which are levied on the enterprises, units and individuals who receive income from agriculture and animal husbandry activities.

In January 2019, the government announced a set of tax reduction policies applicable to small-medium companies, which also applicable to foreign-invested enterprises. First, small-scale VAT taxpayers with monthly sales of less than RMB 100,000 will be exempted from VAT (The threshold for exemption was previously RMB 30,000.). And Second, Companies with Annual Taxable Income less than RMB 3M (The threshold for reduced rate was previously RMB 1M) can enjoy a lower corporate income tax rate between 5-10% (known as the preferential corporate income tax). With the new threshold, more than 95% of Chinese enterprises fit the new criteria for reduced tax rate policy, which is good news for foreign investor who seek to explore the China market.

Please noted that late payment interests computed at the rate of 0.05% per day will be imposed on the amount of tax in arrears. Penalty up to RMB 10,000 may be imposed for failure to file a return and pay tax within the prescribed time limits. In addition, in the case of tax evasion, a penalty ranging from 0.5 to 5 times the amount of tax overdue on the taxpayer or the withholding agent.

Intellectual Property

China joined the World Trade Organization (WTO) in 2001 and is obliged to include international standard intellectual property protection in its national laws. Furthermore, China signed several other international agreements, including the Paris Convention, Berne Convention, Madrid Protocol and Patent Cooperation Treaty.

In China, the protection of intellectual property is based primarily on the Patent Law, the Trademark Law and the Copyright Law. The State Intellectual Property Office (SIPO) is the authority responsible for the registration of Patent and the relevant rights, with its offices at the provincial and municipal level looking after administrative enforcement; Trademarks can be registered with the National Trademarks Office (NTO); and Copyrights are administrated by The National Copyright Administration (NCA). Those governing authorities enforce the law jointly with other relevant local government departments including custom, commerce and police force.

- Trademarks. A sign may be registered as a trademark if it is capable of graphical representation and distinguishing the goods and services of the applicant from those of others. Trying to register a Trademarks which are lack of distinctiveness would likely to be refused by NTO, unless the trademark has acquired a distinctive character as a result of extensive prior use. Infringement of a registered trademark occurs if an identical or confusingly similar mark is used in respect of goods or services confusingly similar or identical to those registered under the trademark. 'Well-known Trademarks' shall enjoy better protection by law. Trademarks may be licensed or transferred. Unregistered trademarks may face difficulty in seeking protection under current Chinese law.

- Patents. To qualify to apply for a patent protection, an invention must be new, which means it is not obvious to a person skilled in the art and with an industrial application. A patent application gives its owner the legal right to exclude others from making, using, selling, and importing an invention for 20 years in China, in exchange for publishing an enabling public disclosure of the invention during the application process. A patent can be licensed or transferred. 'Utility Model' is an alternative to 'Invention' with lower requirement for less protection.
- Registered Designs. Registered Design is protection for designs over the external appearance of objects. A registrable design is a new design defined as features of shape, configuration, and pattern applied to an article by any industrial process, which in the finished article appeal to and are judged by the eye. An article is any article of manufacture and includes any part of an article if that part is made and sold separately. Compare to patent, a registered design enjoys a shorter protection period of 10 years from the date of application.
- Copyright. Copyright protection arises automatically (accordingly Berne Convention for the Protection of Literary and Artistic Works, China as a member) but owner can also take the initiative to register. Ownership of copyright first vests in the author of the work unless made by employees in the course of their employment, in which case copyright vests in the employer in the

absence of an evidence (such as agreement) to the contrary. For commissioned works, unless the contract supports otherwise, the person commissioned remains the copyright owner and the person who commissioned the work enjoys exclusive rights to use the work. Copyright in works can be assigned in writing or licensed provided that the work in question is sufficiently identified. Infringement occurs if a substantial part of a copyright work is copied, published, performed or adapted without the owner's consent. Commercial dealing with infringing copies, including importing, selling, leasing and hiring, may also constitute an infringement.

- Confidential Information. Trade Secret and Confidential information can be protected contractually. Breach of contract and damages can be claimed if there is a misuse or unauthorized disclosure of confidential information. This happens more often in cases with trade secrets stolen and used by ex-employees or OEM manufacturers.

Every year the local authorities run campaign to protect the intellectual property rights of local and foreign businesses, from educating the public, to cracking down on the theft of trade secrets, trademark infringement and patents violations. We suggest clients to engage in a lawyer to design a plan to proactively protect and regularly monitor their interests before the need to seek remedies for IP infringement in China. Taking action against infringement includes coordination with local customs, commercial bureau and courts with complicated legal and administrative procedures.

Trademark infringement is one of the most common type of infringements in China. According to the Trademark Law of China, civil, criminal and administrative actions can all be taken against trademark infringement by trademark registrant or an interested party. A registrant or interested party can use a civil action to obtain an injunction and compensation. In general, civil action can be taken against all kinds of trademark infringement; Administrative action can generally be taken against all kinds of trademark infringement. The major advantage of administrative action is that it can include the confiscation and destruction of infringing goods and related tools, as well as imposing a fine on infringers; and criminal action will be taken to against serious acts of trademark infringement, including counterfeiting registered trademarks, selling commodities carrying counterfeit trademarks and illegally manufacturing registered trademark products with some scales.

Winding up of a Company

There are many reasons why a foreign-invested company might seek to shut down, including financial difficulties, reorganization, merger, relocation or even just a change in business direction. Dissolving and winding up a company in China can be a lengthy process, commonly take one or even two years. Whatever the reasons behind the wind up, there are defined procedures and steps that must be carried out to ensure that the company's final bills are settled, tax is fully paid, and all the company's remaining liabilities and statutory responsibilities are duly discharged. The wind-up procedure ensures there is no adverse effect for either the company or its management. General steps include:

● Informing the Administration of Industry and Commerce (AIC) of the decision to windup an entity.
● Appointing a liquidation committee, this normally involved a legal advisor. The committee's responsibilities include liquidate the assets of the company, preparing financial statements, collecting

from debtor, settling with creditor claims and taxes.
- Issuing a public announcement (on newspaper).
- Submitting a liquidation report to the Board of Directors and relevant authorities.
- Preparing a liquidation audit detailing the financial performance and transactions of the company for the last three years before the date of declaring liquidation.
- Deregistering industry specific permits, licenses, customs certificate and any other approved certificate.
- Settling all outstanding tax and deregistering from local tax bureau.
- Closing all bank accounts and finally deregistering from local Administration of Industry & Commerce.

Bankruptcy of companies are allowed under Chinese law, but not for individuals. Therefore, individuals cannot declare a bankruptcy in China (Individual expatriate must be careful about the adverse meaning of this, although there is a proposal by Government authorities in 2019 to promote the establishment of a bankruptcy system for insolvent individuals step-by-step). According to Enterprise Bankruptcy Law, creditors can apply to the court for bankruptcy liquidation or reorganization of a company if it cannot pay due debts.

Dispute Resolution

While conducting business in China, foreign companies or foreign-invested companies occasionally find themselves run into disputes with local suppliers, partners, employees, customers and even local authorities. The primary ways to resolve a commercial dispute in

China include negotiation, mediation, arbitration and litigation.

Litigation

China adopted a civil law system. Civil Procedure Law and the judicial interpretations on civil procedure are the main rules that govern civil procedure in China, although case law also play a 'guiding role' nowadays and was referred from time to time. There are four levels in the civil court systems, namely, the District Court, the Intermediate Court, the Higher Court, and the Supreme Court. A case can be heard by two courts at different levels, and the decision of the (second) higher court is final. There are specialist courts for intellectual property, maritime and sometimes foreign-related matters.

General procedures can include filing and acceptance of lawsuits, application for an asset protection order (Mareva injunction), serving, pre-trail preparation, jurisdiction appealing, court-directed mediation, case hearing, possible stay or termination of actions, judgments and rulings, appealing procedure and then enforcement of judgments, which normally exceed a period of six months.

In additional to lawyers' fee, litigation fee calculated based on the total sum of the claims in general will be charged by the local courts. Notarization, authentication and translation for out-of-jurisdiction documents are normally required. Lawyers can accept contingent fee arrangement with clients in most cases.

Arbitration

There are professional and independent arbitration bodies in major China cities. China has its own arbitration law and regulation, and is a member of the New York Convention on the Recognition and Enforcement of Foreign Arbitral Awards. The Convention provides a regime for the enforcement and recognition of arbitral awards within contracting state. China has made two reservations: the reciprocity reservation and commercial reservation.

It is worth to highlight that Chinese law recognizes three types of arbitrations: international arbitration, foreign related arbitration and domestic arbitration. If the parties agree to nominate an arbitration panel outside of the PRC and their dispute has no foreign elements, a Chinese court is likely to rule that the choice is an attempt to evade Chinese law and will refuse to recognize the award.

Mediation

China has a long history of mediation, the process of having a respected neutral assisting parties in the resolution of a dispute has existed since ancient times.

There are currently five main types of mediation in China, namely People's Mediation (also known as 'Civil Mediation') conducted by People's Mediation Committees (community mediators); Judicial Mediation conducted by judges; Administrative Mediation conducted by local government officials; Arbitral Mediation conducted by arbitration bodies; and Industry Mediation conducted by respected industrial associations. In particular, judicial mediation as part of civil procedure plays an important role in resolving disputes.

Enforcement of Foreign order

Chinese courts will recognize and enforce foreign judgments or orders based on the ground that either there exist a multilateral or bilateral treaty, or based on the principle of reciprocity.

There are currently thirty something jurisdictions which have concluded a bilateral or multilateral treaty with China that contain provisions of recognition and enforcement of judgment. In addition, China has further Arrangements with Hong Kong and Macau on reciprocal recognition and enforcement of judgments, but not without restrictions and limitations in practice.

PART II - Investing in China

My business in foreign country is running quite well that we may want to expand into China. Are all kinds of business nature welcomed in China?

Sorry, the answer is no. In China, despite policies are continuously opening up to the world, yet there are still some restrictions for foreign investment in relation to the type of business. According to 'Catalogue for the Guidance of Foreign Investment Industries', there are three categories for different industries which are 'encouraged', 'restricted' and 'prohibited'. (For instance, industries producing baby food, goods for elderly or healthcare products are encouraged; industries for wines, direct marketing, online sales are restricted; industries for mailing and courier services, free educational institution, publishers for books, newspapers and magazines are prohibited.) Any foreign-related investment not listed in these three categories are generally considered to be 'allowed' category. It differs from different regions and different industries, the rules and restrictions may vary too. For instance, the Chinese government had amended the 'Catalogue of Priority Industries for Foreign Investment in Central and Western China' in 2013 & 2017 (expired). For expatriates who wants to invest in China, there are indeed more guidelines and policies worth his attention.

Case Sharing: Removing the foreign ownership limit in firms providing securities and fund management services

Speaking in a forum in 2019, Yi Gang, governor of the People's Bank of China, said the central bank would support a pilot program to remove the foreign ownership limit in firms providing securities and fund management services. He highlighted capital market reform plans, include removing of limit on foreign ownership of domestic financial institutions.

Sharing in the same occasion, Yi Huiman, chairman of the China Securities Regulatory Commission (CSRC), said he would push forward with plans to liberalize market access in nine areas. These included a further relaxation to foreign investors on access to capital markets, a broadening of cross-border investment channels and targets, and measures to facilitate trading and fundraising.

For concessionary measures in tax, in general, the preferential terms and measures to attract foreign-investment enterprises are adjusting and diminishing. In terms of profit tax for corporations, there is less and less differentiation between domestic and foreign-funded enterprises, but in some cases foreign enterprises still enjoy some attractive benefits. Take an example, for corporation that are recognized as high-tech enterprises can enjoy preferential treatment of corporate income tax rate of 15%. In addition, there are so-called 'double-soft identification', in which the 'Soft' refers to software companies and software products. Enterprises for software and software products with proper identification and certification can enjoy taxation concessionary policies (2 Exemptions and 3 Reductions years). Local governments may further give certain tax discounts depending on the specific location of the company. For example, a foreign enterprise that is qualified to run its business in Shenzhen Qianhai or it is of the 'encouraged' category industry in the western region, these kinds of foreign investor can apply for a lower tax rate of 15% and sometimes other supporting terms.

- Foreign Investment Law of the People's Republic of China, 2020
- Special Administrative Measures (Negative List) for the Access of Foreign Investment (2019)
- Catalogue of Industries for Guiding Foreign Investment, revised 2017
- Administrative Measures for Approval and Record-filing of Foreign Investment Projects, 2014

A friend recommended me to invest into a Chinese Company for its shares, what are the major areas I should be aware of?

The China's economic growth rapidly, especially under the 'One Belt, One Road'strategic economic policy, many China Enterprises have vast potential in development. Yet it can still be very risky in terms of investment, risk associated with cross-border mergers and acquisitions including but not limited to contract risk, financial risk, asset risk, customer risk, employee risk, confidentiality risk, credit risk, legal and litigation risk, and so on. Therefore, before investing in a Chinese company, in addition to understanding the company's legal status, management status, business status, and financial status, investors should conduct a comprehensive business investigation of the company. Clients would normally hire Chinese lawyers to conduct due diligence in order to reduce and control transaction risks. A due diligence usually includes:

- Checking the registration information, license and business qualification of relevant entities of the enterprise;
- Checking the management structure, corporate governance,

shareholder structure, paid-up capital and historical change of capital, stocks and shares transfer history of target;
- Reviewing the financial information of target. In particular related to major assets of the enterprise including the certificates and permits for real estate property, land use and facilities;
- Checking validity of contract rights, IP rights and other resources rights of the enterprise;
- Reviewing related parties' transaction;
- Checking account receivable and payable status of target. Particularly all the liability in relation to loan, debts and guarantee;
- Checking major contracts relation and agreement of target with its business partners, suppliers, clients and related parties;
- Checking target if any disputes with connected parties, and court proceeding progress;
- Checking the benefits and taxation privileges that the enterprise is enjoying;
- Checking if any warning and punishment imposed by government, industrial bureaus, environmental bureau and tax authority to target;
- Checking target in relation to compliance of employee relation with employment-related rules, regulations and policies.

Case Sharing: A supplier failed in due diligence

In 2012, a renowned European company conducted due diligence on a potential supplier company in China. Investigation results showed more than a dozen of lawsuits were filed against this supplier company mainly for sales contract disputes and loan. On top of this, there was a persistent problem of overdue and unpaid wages with the factory's workers. The factory production efficiency was therefore low while workers constantly focused in urging for their salaries rather than working hard. The results through due diligence conducted suggested that the supplier company might has financially unstable the worth this European company to think twice before entering into the high-risk cooperation.

- China Company Law of the People's Republic of China, revised 2018
- Provisions of the Supreme People's Court on Several Issues Concerning the Trial of Disputes over Foreign-funded Enterprises (I), 2010

What are the fundamentals for start doing business in China?

China is expected to surpass U.S. as the world's largest retail market from 2019 and onwards. According to a news report, China is now underscoring the growing middle class, hoping to shift the country into a consumer-driven economy.

When doing research or googling about the Chinese market, there are lots of messages popping up telling you the importance of 'guanxi' (relationship), 'mianzi' (face) and all sorts of cultural differences for doing business in China. As a lawyer, I would say the key points below are equally important:

1. Get a valid legal entity

If you are more than just a business traveller paying visits to your Chinese suppliers placing orders with a fixed office location and a plan to recruit your first assistant, you are suggested to register your own Chinese entity. It can be a Wholly Foreign Owned Entity (WFOE) as limited company, a joint venture, or a representative office in China. Nowadays the rules in relation to the paid-up capital for company registry has been relaxed, i.e. a company in general industries can be registered with capital of RMB 1.

2. Follow local employment laws strictly

China's employment laws are comprehensive and has national, provincial, and local levels. If you are not complying with all levels of rules and regulations, your company could easily get into trouble. The system is more complex than you can imagine such as the rules in relation to firing a staff, compensation for termination, paying overtime wages, holiday arrangements, social insurance calculations and so on. Therefore, it is wise for you to consult your Chinese lawyer before issuing your first employment contract.

3. Make sure you have enforceable contracts

Companies shall keep valid contracts for most of their business activities, whereas the court expects a contract in writing and properly signed, even though a verbal one or something in email is not against the rule. And, a contract in Chinese will save you some troubles. Do not simply jump into conclusion that it is better if the jurisdiction is in your hometown. Our experience tells that local judgment is far more effective than a foreign one in terms of enforcement and especially when your counterparty is in China.

4. Protect your intellectual property

Protection of your intellectual property includes protecting your trademarks, patents, and copyrights. In China, the rules of first-come-first-serve rule is adopted in general. It is crucial that you would register your rights in China before you actually start any production or promotion activities.

5. Pay tax

Death and taxes are inevitable and unavoidable in life. This is of course, also the case in China. Interest and penalties will be imposed if anyone fail to pay tax in China. For serious tax evasion, criminal law in China will be applied.

6. Watch out for different industry rules

Rules for the same industry may vary in different countries. Don't just ignore or go with your common sense even if you are veteran. In China, the Chinese law in relation to customs, marketing, competition, antitrust, consumer rights can be a lot different from that of other countries.

7. Do not engage in unlawful activities

Despite all the rumors, engaging in unlawful activities is not a pre-requisite for being success in doing business in China. Properly and diligently keep your account and book according to rules. If someone telling you a bribe is required, check with your Chinese partner or your lawyer.

Case Sharing: The rapid growth of a new local brand in two years' time, thanks to the substantially larger middle-class population in China

According to news in 2018, a Chinese makeup company Perfect Diary announced it was the first cosmetics brand to achieve sales volume of more than RMB 100 million during the 11 November online shopping campaign (a 24 hours annual shopping activity on Taobao and Tmall e-commerce platform).

The makeup company was setup in 2016 and launched on Alibaba's Tmall e-commerce platform. The start-up targets the generation born in the mid-1990s with marketing campaigns featuring popular celebrities and top models. The company is also launching physical stores, with plans to quadruple its physical stores to 40 by the end of 2019, and 600 by 2022.

- Foreign Investment Law of the People's Republic of China, 2020
- Labor Law of the People's Republic of China (2018 Amendment)
- Labor Contract Law of the People's Republic of China (2012 Amendment)
- Regulation on the Implementation of the Enterprise Income Tax Law of the People's Republic of China (2019 Amendment)

What are the risks of doing business without having a proper entity?

Many expatriates are tempted start doing business straight away without having a proper entity in China. However, there are severe risks for those who do not register company and start doing business. Below are some good reasons to have a proper entity for doing business in China:

1. Legal protection

One of the very good reasons to register a business is to protect yourself. The protection level is made effective depending on the company structure. For instance, setting up a limited liability company will impose a limit to your personal liability against debts and lawsuits filed of your company. Legal protection is very crucial when things go wrong as they sometimes will.

2. Intellectual property (IP) protection

If your business is not registered, your company's name cannot be trademarked. As a result, it's very easy for competitors to copy your branding and steal your customers, leaving you defenseless. Worse still, the first-come-first-serve basis of IP law in China neglects how long the business has been running. There were many cases where someone with bad intention will register all sorts of business names and logos when (or actually, before) you enter the Chinese market and wait until you become successful to force you ceasing trading or ask for monetary compensation.

3. Access to necessary services and infrastructure

Another huge issue of doing business in China without registering your company is the practical constraints on the capability for you to run your business. For example, if you do not register your company, you are unable to issue official invoices (Fapiao) and resulted in limiting your client base as almost all Chinese companies require Fapiao with your official company name printed when they work with you. You may also run in similar Fapiao problem when you work with your suppliers and such hurdles may be fatal to the growth of your company and affect the smoothness and convenience in operation. Without a legally registered company, you may also encounter difficulties when accessing the banking services such as opening a bank account or applying loan from banks. The scope of services from the bank will become very limited to you as an expatriate. Last but not least, if you run your business without registering a company in China, you are actually operating your business outside the official system and thus your 'employees' may not be able to enjoy the social welfare and hinder the hiring opportunity.

4. Avoiding legal liabilities

Aside from the practical limitations imposed to the operation of your business, it is an act to break the Chinese law if you do not register your business in China when doing business. The consequences of breaking such law include:

- Being fined. Individuals will be fined under Tax Law, Business Registration Law and Labor Law. Application of law may vary depending on where your business is located and scale of operation. The fine can be heavy.
- Suspension of operations. A business found to be operating without proper license will be ordered to suspend its operation.
- Deportation. Owners of business without registering in China may be deported and banned from doing business in China permanently.
- In extreme cases or severe circumstances, individual doing business in China without registering a company may be subjected to criminal charges. This would happen especially when the business is involved in sales of products causing significant harm to the public. (For example, illegal and unregulated manufacturing of food and drugs)

If you are working as a freelancer with only a few other partners or staff without a need of a registered office, you may be able to keep your business running in low profile while good-enough in finding and retaining a few clients to sustain the business. However, if you are serious about the growth of your business, you shall register your business properly as soon as possible.

- Foreign Investment Law of the People's Republic of China, 2020
- China Company Law of the People's Republic of China, revised 2018

Why foreign investor should start with Hong Kong before entering into China market?

During the incident 'Huawei CFO Meng Wanzhou arrested in Canada, faces extradition to United States' since Dec 2018, we see from news that U.S. government immediately imposed travel warning for China, and coincidently Canadians were detained for breaking laws in China, so on and so forth.

From time to time, expatriates keep asking questions about the identity that they should carry when they run a business in China. Shall one go into China as a US invested company (WFOE) directly? Depends on situations of individual clients, but one popular arrangement is to form a new company in Hong Kong first and then using this Hong Kong company as a holding company (or, Special Purpose Vehicle, SPV) to control the China entity and local business.

Hong Kong is one of the quickest locations to incorporate a business. Hong Kong company is often used as SPV to invest in China. Investors from Europe and North America (and historically, Japan) will especially choose to register a Hong Kong company as a SPV to invest in China, with simple reason to reduce the potential risk arise from their identity of their own country. In fact, starting with a Hong Kong holding company is the most common and an efficient structure for foreign investment into China while Hong Kong has always been the preferred jurisdiction for structuring both China inbound and outbound investments.

Using a Hong Kong holding company for Chinese investment, in most cases offer foreign investors more protection than via a direct shareholding in a Chinese company (or Joint venture), where ownership is shared with a local Chinese partner. Structuring a joint venture at the Hong Kong level may simply offer greater flexibility and less risk for investors.

In addition, the procedures of transferring or restructuring the shareholdings in China which requires compliance with Chinese regulations and cooperation of local authorities could sometimes be lengthy when it is compared to the clearer procedures in Hong Kong.

The tax agreement between Hong Kong and Mainland China pave way for the ease of investing in China through a Hong Kong company. The Closer Economic Partnership Arrangement (CEPA) which brought into effect at the beginning of 2004 provides Hong Kong entity investing in Mainland China with extra and exclusive market access benefits.

Many investors prefer having their contracts and disputes governed under their familiar Hong Kong (common) law and the jurisdiction of Hong Kong courts to Chinese (civil) law and People's Courts, which sometimes make sense. Moreover, the tax rates in Hong Kong may be close to the lowest in the globe. It provides investors a very simple and predictable tax regime.

- Mainland and Hong Kong Closer Economic Partnership Arrangement (CEPA), 2003

How shall I choose between WFOE and RO for my business?

This is a frequently asked question. The major differences between a Wholly Foreign-Owned Enterprise (WFOE) and Representative Office (RO) are as follows:

1. Scope of Business

WFOEs are allowed in servicing, trading, manufacturing, and nowadays most industries except those restricted or require prior approval. A RO cannot carry out business in its own name.

2. Legal position

A RO is not a legal entity in China, being a branch of a foreign organization, a RO is not an independent legal person and is not allowed to generate sales, sign contract, nor stock products. A WFOE is a local independent legal entity.

3. Register Capital

A WFOE is a limited liability company, meaning that the liability of the shareholders is limited to the assets they brought to the business with a defined register capital. In practice, the official requirements for registered capital vary by industry and region. Say, a minimum of RMB 500,000 or RMB 1million registered capital is a common starting point for general industries. (China is currently implementing a zero registered capital rule for domestic companies under the revised company law, but that still not yet fully applied to WFOEs and special industries.)

A RO as its name is only a representative of a foreign company and therefore do not require to have its own register capital.

4. Staff Arrangement

A RO can only employ people through government licensed third party labor agency. A WFOE do not have this limitation.

5. Tax

ROs are taxed on running expense, for example, a flat rate of 12% tax on expenses. WFOEs are taxed in similar way as domestic companies, who can make profits and issue local invoices (Fapiao) in RMB to its customers (which are crucial as invoices are the basis for obtaining tax deductions in China). WFOE may sometimes enjoy tax relief policy on profit compare to its domestic counterparts (but again depends on location and industry).

6. Duration

A WFOE registration normally valid for 10 years or above and renewable, while that for a RO starting from 1 year. The termination or deregistration procedure for a RO is simpler than that for a WFOE who need to follow more lengthy winding up procedures like its domestic counterpart.

Case Sharing: China's giant middle class supports the growth of Multinational companies and start-ups

According to report, McKinsey analysis indicates the Chinese middle class could reach 550 million in three years — more than one-and-a-half times the entire U.S. population in 2019, and MNC are trying to tap the massive market. Here are some quotes from the news:

- 'Consumption overall is robust, and you see what is driving that, it's new consumers entering the middle class, and that is the primary driver of growth in the China market,' Daniel Zipser, senior partner at McKinsey, said in a phone interview with CNBC reporter, 2019.
- American electric car maker Tesla has registered a wholly-owned construction company in China, with the company's scope of activities including architectural design, construction and building materials. Zhu Xiaotong, a Tesla executive in China, was listed as the construction company's legal representative. Tesla aims to produce at least 1,000 Model 3s a week from the new factory by the end of 2019 to boost sales in the world's biggest auto market and avoid China's higher import tariffs imposed on U.S. cars, and the plant's mass production schedule is crucial for Tesla's hopes of reaching its total production rate at an annualized 500,000 vehicles by the end of 2019. The USD 2 billion factory is Tesla's first car manufacturing site overseas and is China's first fully foreign-owned car plant, is a reflection of China government's broader shift to open up its car market. Local authorities have offered assistance to speed up construction, and excluded Tesla models from a 10% car purchase tax.
- Walmart sees its chance now as well. The American retail giant has been in China for more than 20 years, but it is stepping up investment in the country with plans to build at least 14 more

Sam's Club membership stores by 2022, for a total of 40 to 45 locations.
- Kentucky Fried Chicken parent Yum China said it has 'invested heavily' in the 'booming' coffee market, becoming the second largest retailer by cups sold at more than 90 million servings.

■ Foreign Investment Law of the People's Republic of China, 2020
■ Regulation on the Administration of Registration of Resident Representative Offices of Foreign Enterprises (2018 Amendment)

How can one transfer money in and out of China?

From time to time there are enquires from clients about how to get money into and out of China properly. This is not only just a concern with expatriates, with the 'one belt, one road' strategy, there are increasing number of Chinese enterprises 'going out'. However, the existence of numerous underground banks and agencies might already hint this is not always that convenient in practice.

- Transferring money into China

In reality, we encounter relatively less enquiries about how to transfer money into China, as the application process for transferring money into China is relatively simpler via foreign investment fund, setting up China entities, Cross-border contract remittance or even someone will bring cash to China personally. So, transferring money into China is relatively simple.

Officially, inward remittance can be conducted in accordance with the usual banking practices. Recipient in China need to provide the Chinese bank a valid contract (such as purchase of services or goods) together with, proper invoice, tax receipt, then one can convert the USD into Renminbi (RMB) for local use. I suggest one to confirm his Chinese counterparts to bare and take care of the tax imposed before the transfer.

RMB remittance with bank is only available to corporate customer under the scope of 'Renminbi for Trade Settlement Services'. For RMB remittances to and from the Chinese counterparts, the Chinese authorities and Chinese banks will be responsible for reviewing whether the transaction is in compliance with the relevant rules and requirements of the Chinese authorities, which means more document and complications.

If you are investing into China, upon setting up a new company (WFOE) or new project in China, and you can transfer your money (USD or RMB) into a designated Chinese company bank account as capital injection. There is no limit for your investment amount, and the procedure shall be smooth in general.

Another convenient way of transferring small sum of money cross-border between individuals is through agent such as West Union. It is simple, fast, and without the need of a lot of information or professional assistance.

Transfer from a Hong Kong bank account into China is generally more flexible and convenience.

- Transferring money out of China

Shall we bring lots of cash when crossing the border? Or using illegal remittance company? Or purchasing financial products in

Hong Kong with credit cards? Or getting cash from ATM machine in overseas or buying luxury products to cash back by selling them? No! All the above-mentioned ways are not our recommendations. (We would also advise everyone about their legal risks)

The underlying questions of transferring money out of China is actually the issue about how an individual send over USD 50,000 out of China as USD 50,000 is the annual limit per individual with a local Chinese ID card for general purpose and free use.

We have heard cases about individuals transferring USD 500,000 for the purpose of US immigration by way of asking 10 friends or relatives to transfer their own personal limit of USD 50,000 at the bank to his designated account.

Although there were sources said that QDII (Qualified Domestic Institutional Investors) will consider loosen the limit of the USD 50,000 per year per individual, started in selected cities, nothing was officially released so far. So, at the moment, one still need government approval in advance to transfer out of China for any amount exceeding USD 50,000. Regulations do state that procedure for the filing case will be completed in three-days-time with Department of Commerce (outward investment and economic cooperation sector), however, in practice, many cases will take longer and involve applications with other government bodies such as State Administration of Foreign Exchange (SAFE), National Development and Reform Commission, and also State-owned Assets Supervision and Administration Commission (SASAC) for state-owned related enterprise. For sensitive project, you will expect to provide more thorough information and take even longer for the assessment.

It may be logical to think if you are better connected and with project supported at the local level, or you are wiring a smaller lump sum of money, approval should be easier to obtain.

In addition, for Foreign Enterprise which had applied and registered for foreign remittance to transfer profits to overseas in accordance with the regulations, the bank will conduct due diligence on the board resolution on such single profit transfer, tax filing forms in relation to relevant law and regulations. Applications can be made after due diligence has been conducted.

So as the rule, any transfer made without approval is a violation of Chinese law. To get around the restrictions, many Chinese companies do make their overseas investments with funds (income) already located outside of China, mostly in Hong Kong, BVI or Cayman Islands etc.

And for our expatriate friends, obviously it is illegal to work in China without a work permit or paying tax. It also impacts on realizing or transferring the money you have earned, so, double check your employment contract terms.

Finally, be aware of illegal China investment, since some industries are still relatively restricted to foreign investors, including telecoms, insurance, banking, publishing and transportation. It may be easy to get money into China illegally, but it is much more difficult to get the money out from your illegal investments. Make sure you are clear with the nature of the project, checking all the pre-approval paper work (have your lawyer doing due diligence) and transfer money into China in a proper way, and do not just believe in high-level involvement or promises from individual senior official, because by the time when you are having a problem, he won't be there testifying.

Case Sharing: Hundreds arrested in China crackdown on underground banks

The cash involved in the illegal banking operations busted amounted to USD 131 billion, according to a report. China's police authority said it busted more than 380 'underground banks'in 2016, involving over RMB 900 billion (USD 131 billion) as the authorities attempt to stem an exodus of cash flowing out of the country.

In 2019, China has introduced new jail terms for operators of underground banks that illegally helping people in China transfer money out of the country to buy property overseas. The Supreme People's Court introduced a stricter penalties for illegal currency exchanges, to stop capital from leaving the country without proper applications. The law imposes jail terms of five years or more for offenders, would target the operators of underground banks that facilitate illegal foreign exchange and cross-border trading.

Under the new rules, illegal foreign currency transactions of more than RMB 5 million (USD 740,000) or those which generated illegal profits of more than RMB 100,000, would be treated as a serious violation. The punishment would be up to five years in prison and fines of up to five times the profit made on the transaction. Jail terms of more than five years would be imposed for cases involving more than RMB 25 million or transactions generating more than RMB 500,000.

- Measures for the Administration of Overseas Investment of Enterprises,2018
- Measures for the Administration of Individual Foreign Exchange, 2007

- Policy Q&A of the State Administration of Foreign Exchange on Some Foreign Exchange Management Business, 2019
- Notice of the State Administration of Foreign Exchange on Issuing the Provisions on the Foreign Exchange Administration of the Overseas Direct Investment of Domestic Institutions, 2009

As an owner of foreign company, shall I be the legal representative of our China subsidiary?

Setting up a limited company to do business in China is one of the most common practice. To set up a limited company, the requirement is to have at least one adult shareholder and director to provide a registered address and to pay a designated capital. In China, there are two types of company capital, namely, domestic capital and foreign capital. Limited liability companies in China is similar in nature to the Limited Company in western world. Yet, they are still different from the Limited Company in western world in terms of equity and management rights. Among all the differences, the most distinctive one is about the adoption of Legal Representative System of the China companies. A legal representative refers to the person in charge who exercises the functions and powers on behalf of the legal entity (company) in accordance with the law or the articles of association. In general, it cannot be an ordinary employee and can only be acted by the chairman, executive director or manager. Legal representative plays an important role in a company with significant power and also responsibility.

Case Sharing: Mr. Li is legally responsible for being the 'Nominated-Legal-Representative' of a company

Mr. Li, who is in his 60s, retired from the management position of a big corporation and being invited by his friend to be the legal representative of a China company established by Mr. Wang. It is agreed that Mr. Li does not required to work nor invest any money and he can keep the 'dry stock' (meaning receiving profit sharing and holding stock share of the company without paying capital). It is promised that if there are any problems arise in the future, all the liability will go to Mr. Wang and Mr. Li shall not be liable. They put it down on paper.

In the first few years, the company runs well with decent performance and track record and thus Mr. Li received bonus and profit sharing from the company. Yet since 2015, prosecutors and police kept looking for Mr. Li for assistance in investigation and claimed that Mr. Li is liable for the legal responsibility for a commercial crime. Mr. Li was asked to assist in the investigation. All of a sudden, Mr. Li was facing legal risks along with civil liabilities, administrative liabilities and criminal liabilities. We would like to remind our readers that the agreement between Li and Wang in relation to 'the limited liability on operations and management for being a Nominated-Legal-Representative'was only effective internally. Such agreement is only valid between the two parties internally, but the agreement has no legal effect externally.

- Foreign Investment Law of the People's Republic of China, 2020
- China Company Law of the People's Republic of China, revised 2018
- Regulation of the People's Republic of China on the Administration of Company Registration (2016 Revision)

What should be paid attention to when Foreign-invested Enterprise in China hiring Chinese employees?

The process of foreign-invested enterprises hiring Chinese domestic employees should be the same as Chinese companies hiring Chinese employees. There are no special restrictions for foreign-invested enterprises, and both of them must follow the rules of 'sign contract before work'which means employers must sign employment contracts with employees before employees report for duty. Please note that all the employment contracts must be drafted based on the 'Labor Law' and 'Labor Contract Law' in China. In addition, should Foreign-invested enterprise hire foreign employees, applications for work permits and visas are required. Among all the rules, according to the 'Labor Contract Law' of the China, Employers will be fined for double compensation and liability if no employment contracts had been signed within 30days the employees report for duty. The China regulatory authorities impose various regulations in relation to the internal management of the employees of the enterprise, it is recommended that employers should hire professionals to take responsibilities in hiring and managing employees.

In case of disputes arise between the employers and employees, arbitration committee formed for labor disputes will be the first stop. Both employer and employee can appoint lawyers to represent them. If the party disagrees on the arbitral award, they may further take the case to the court in most situations.

Case Sharing: Foreign-invested Enterprise being severely penalized for overtime work

In 2007, investigation found that many Beijing Olympic product licensed manufacturers had violated the 'Labor Law' in relation to labor issues in Guangdong area. In one of the reporting, according to Shenzhen Municipal Labor and Social Security Bureau spokesman, two of the firms among all the licensed Olympic souvenirs licensed manufacturers had instructed their employees to work long hours and one failed to pay overtime compensation to employees. Investigations show that there were 2,779 of the 3,000 employees were each forced to work 36 extra hours in May 2007, violating the overtime hours requirement of the Labor Law while at the other firm, 1,779 of the 2,600 staff were each forced to work 60 to 100 extra hours. The two firms were fined about RMB 833,700 and RMB 533,700 respectively, equivalent to RMB 300 for each employee.

- Labor Law of the People's Republic of China (2018 Amendment)
- Labor Contract Law of the People's Republic of China (2012 Amendment)

What are the arrangements for Foreign-invested Enterprises in China to hire expatriates as employees?

Since the economic development of China and the National strategies to 'go global' and 'attract foreign investment', there was a rising trend of expatriates working in China, in particular in the first-tier big coastal cities. According to a media reports in 2015, over 20,000 expatriates and foreigners are permanently residing in Shenzhen while over 1 million of them are temporarily living in Shenzhen, and more than 0.46 million foreigners living in Shanghai. There is a rising trend for expatriates working and living in China and naturally disputes in relation to foreigners-related employment contracts are also climbing. So how should companies and enterprises protect their rights and interests?

1. Prepare a clear contract with concise content

According to Decision of the **Ministry of Human Resources and Social Security on Amending the Provisions on the Employment Administration of Aliens in China (2017) (the Provisions on the Employment of Foreigners in China (2010 Amendment))**, the employment period of foreign-related labor contracts must be a fixed term, and the maximum period must not exceed five years. In addition, companies should pay attention to the relevant details of the contract, including the company must pay attention to the foreigner's name and signature should be consistent with the name and signature of the passport and the employment permit when signing a written contract with the foreigner. If a contract is found to be unsigned, the company will face the risk of paying double wages and administrative penalties. If a foreigner refuses to sign a labor contract, the enterprise shall notify the foreigner in writing to terminate the labor relationship within one month from the date of employment. Recruiting an employee without a contract will be subjected to compensation to employee and penalty from authority.

2. Apply for employment permit and visa according to rules and regulations

Enterprises should follow regulations to apply employment visa and relevant annual review applications for their foreign employees. If employment visa and annual review applications are missing or any visas or permits are used beyond the restricted scope or the employment entity is inconsistent with what is shown on the employment permit, the enterprise may constitute illegal employment and violate the laws related to the Exit and Entry Administration which stipulates that any companies employ foreigners privately, and those who are illegally employed by foreigners shall be fined not less than RMB 5,000 but not more than RMB 20,000; For serious offence, employers shall be detained for at least 5 days but not more than 15 days, and pay a fine of RMB 5000 but not more than RMB 20,000. For those who illegally introduce foreigners to be employed in China, they will be fined for RMB 5000 per foreigner but not over RMB 50000 in total. For employment agencies illegally introducing foreigners for employment in China, a fine of RMB 5000 per employees shall be enforced but not exceeding RMB 100,000 in total. If there is any illegal income, all the illegal income shall be confiscated.

3. Enroll for social security

Expatriates working in China shall acquire full coverage of social security insurance like every other employee working in China.

China has signed social security recognition related agreement with some countries. For example, expatriates from Germany and South Korea who can provide their guarantees from their home countries, German employees do not need to pay pension insurance and unemployment insurance, Korean employees do not need to pay pension insurance, and others should be paid in China. For a general expatriate, one will need to subscribe social insurance in full like a local employee. Enterprises shall handle and pay social security insurance for expatriates based on the 'Interim Measures for Participation in Social Insurance for Foreigners Employed in China', 'Taiwan Hong Kong and Macau Residents Employment Management Regulations in the Mainland'. If a company does not apply for social security and insurance for foreign employees, it shall pay the late payment fee and pay the fine in accordance with the provisions of the Social Insurance Law.

4. Employ staff with the right entity

Enterprise shall ensure consistency for the name of the entity for its staff use for admin, daily work and labor contract, where the name of the entity used must be the same as the registration. Otherwise, condition such as the working hour record and obligations stipulated in the employment contract may not be made into effect to their employees. In addition, enterprise not using a proper entity name will risk themselves for having invalid employment contract and thus risk themselves to pay for double wages to their employees as well as being fined by labor authority. In case of forgery, alteration, fraudulent use, transfer or sales of employment permit, punishment will be enforced to three parties, namely the foreign employee, the enterprise who is the employer and the company who apply the employment permit. If serious offences occur, criminal liabilities may be charged.

5. Provide Staff Guidebook and Daily Work Manual in translated or English versions

Enterprise shall provide its staff with a Staff Guidebook with clear definitions and detailed execution standards and procedures of operation so that all employees can confirmed their understanding by their signatures. According to experience of author, there are always only Chinese version available with China companies for most of the time. If enterprises hiring foreign employees, it is strongly suggested that they will prepare staff guidebook, daily work manuals, daily internal notices and correspondences, HR-related documents, salary schemes and all kind of daily work communication in English so that the foreign employees can fully comprehend the update and working arrangement of the enterprises. When labor disputes arise or termination of contract is needed for a foreign employee, it would be a legal risk to enterprises when they did not fulfil their obligation in properly informing their employees about the details of their employment. It is an effective way to minimize the labor dispute if enterprises can provide very clear and defined guidelines and content of employment to their foreign employees in foreign language which they can comprehend.

6. Be aware that China law shall apply

Although in accordance with the provisions of Contract Law in China, involving parties can choose the jurisdiction to resolve the disputes when it is a foreign-related matter. However, there are exceptions that foreign-invested companies should be pay attention to. Exceptions include for circumstances and matters in relation to Labor Law, Labor Contract Law and Regulations governing foreigners employed in China, all these laws apply and based on the legal principle of territorial jurisdiction. That is, when labor dispute arises, the labor law of People's Republic of China applies. A usual practice for multinational corporations (MNCs) is to use the same identical employment contract template for all the employees worldwide BUT alongside with an extra one setting out rules and guidelines in accordance with Labor Law in China with Chinese version or Bilingual versions in order to comply with local rules and minimize the legal risk when labor dispute arises.

7. Make it clear for renewal of contracts arrangement with foreign employees

Before the end date of the employment contract, employers shall discuss with employees for contract renewal. For instance, a 'Labor Contract Renewal Proposal' will free the enterprise from risk to pay extra monetary compensation to its employees in case the employees do not want to renew any further contracts with the enterprise. Once a 'Labor Contract Renewal Proposal' is signed by employee, the employer shall be exempted from paying compensation relating to initiating a termination of contract, even the employee change his mind later and decide not to continue his service with the company.

Enterprise shall pay attention that the employment permit will be invalid upon the expiration date of the employment contract. If any renewal of employment contract applies, the enterprise is required to further register for the employment permit before entering a new employment contract. In case that the employment permit expires while the employment contract is still in effect, employers shall renew the employment permit 30 days before the expiration date. If registration of renewal for the employment permit is not made, the permit will be automatically be invalid upon the expiration date. It is an offence if any of the employees are using expired or invalid employment permits. If there is any illegal employment, both the employers and employees shall be liable to penalties.

The above rules are mainly for foreigners who work in China and have foreign nationality. They are also generally applicable to the employment of residents from Taiwan, Hong Kong and Macau in the China. However, the employment arrangements for employees from Hong Kong, Macau and Taiwan should refer to the relevant special regulations on Regulations on Employment Management of Taiwan, Hong Kong and Macau Residents in the Mainland.

- Decision of the Ministry of Human Resources and Social Security on Amending the Provisions on the Employment Administration of Aliens in China (2017)
- The Provisions on the Employment of Foreigners in China (2010 Amendment)
- Exit and Entry Administration of the People's Republic of China, 2012
- Social Insurance Law of the People's Republic of China (2018 Amendment)

Can an employer freely fire an employee during probation period?

Of course not. Employers cannot casually terminate the employment of its employees throughout the employment contract period, and enterprise shall normally pay economic compensation to employee for terminating a labor contract.

Some bosses or human resources managers would believe that firing a staff during probationary period is an easy task (they just need a sentence: 'You are fired!???'). According to Chinese law, employers are required to provide proof and evidence to fire a staff even during probationary period. Proof and evidence from the employer shall include a written employment terms explained to the employees during the hiring process and a list of possible 'under-performance indicators' in labor contract for employees the measure during probationary period. Otherwise, the company will face legal risks upon termination with employees and shall be liable to compensation the employees.

Case Sharing: Employee Kai X shall be liable for illegal termination of labor contract

Company: Kai X Technology (Shenzhen) Co., Ltd.

Employee: Chen X-qiao.

Appellant Kai X Technology (Shenzhen) Co., Ltd. filed an appeal with Shenzhen Baoan District People's Court (2015) against Civil Judgment No. 290.

The Court held that the facts about the relations of Chen X-qiao and Kai X Technology (Shenzhen) Co., Ltd was clear. The legitimate rights and interests of both parties were protected by the Labor Law and regulations.

The focus of the dispute in this case is whether Kai X Technology (Shenzhen) Co., Ltd. has illegally terminated the labor contract with Chen X-qiao. Kai X Technology (Shenzhen) Co., Ltd. proposed that Chen X-qiao should be dismissed on Dec. 11, 2014 in accordance with the company's management regulations because of his frequent failures and serious negligence causing monetary losses to the company and violating the recruitment requirements during the probation period. Chen disagreed and believed that his dismissal and termination on 13 Dec 2014 was illegal as the agreed probationary period should be end on 12 Dec 2014, therefore the termination was after the probationary period.

The court held that Kai X Technology failed to provide valid proof in relation to the frequent failures and serious negligence of Chen which caused substantial monetary loss to the company. The Court also held that Kai X Technology failed to prove its management guidelines to employees as well as its responsibility to make known to the employees via notice, therefore Kai X Technology shall be liable for not providing enough proof and bare the legal consequences. Thus, the Court held that whether or not Chen was terminated during the probationary period, Kai X Technology shall be liable for illegal termination of labor contract. Kai X Technology shall pay Chen relative compensation arise from illegal termination.

We advise that the human resources department or personnel of the Chinese Enterprise shall keep original record of all the signed employment contracts and the details for every employee. The employment contacts shall be listed with details of Job Description (JD) and Key Performance Indicator (KPI). It is also advised that the company shall indicate clearly and communicate to the employees about the start date and end date of the probationary period and whether or not it is both days inclusive; how the employees should considered as passing the probationary period within the defined time and date with relevant department or through tests, etc. All these regulations shall be explained to the employees and signed by them as acknowledgment. It is also advised that employer shall record the performance of every employees from time to time during the probationary period. Records shall be kept carefully, and copies should be made to the employees.

Employers in China shall be cautious with the rules and regulations in relation to termination of employees in accordance to the Labor Law. In general, there are three kinds of termination according to the Labor Law as follows:

1. In the following circumstances, employers can terminate its employment contract with an employee with immediate effect:

- Prove that the employee is unable to satisfy the employment terms;
- The employee seriously violate the rules, regulations and employment guidelines of the employer;
- Serious negligence of the employee which leads to substantial and significant monetary loss of the employer;
- The employee is convicted for criminal offences.

2. In the following circumstances, employers shall first provide the employee with 30-day notice:

- The employee cannot perform his / her original duties, or any other new duties assigned by the employer after recovering from a sickness or injuries out of work;
- The employee is lack of capability to perform the duties assigned by the employer and fail to perform even the employer has rearranged other position and duties for the employee.
- Significant and major changes happened causing the

situation and environment differs from the details of the employment contract, forbidding the company to carry on its employment and new terms cannot be agreed between the employer and the employee. Employer shall pay compensation to the employee if the employer terminates the employment contract based on the above-mentioned three circumstances.

3. Termination due to economic difficulties of the employer such as adverse difficulties in operation or bankruptcy. The employer shall inform the authorities, the employees, and labor association or representative 30 days prior to the termination with compensation paid to every employee. In case disputes arise between employer and the employee, one can apply for mediation, arbitration or litigation to solve the problem. In China, most of the disputes in relation to employer and employee related to the violation of employment contract, wages, leave arrangement, social security insurance. As the employer is liable to provide evidence and proof in a dispute at court, it is suggested that employers shall seek legal assistant about drafting of employment contract, methodology in keeping proper attendance records, the proper and legal way of paying wages and all other rules and regulations about staff management arrangement. Employers are advised that good records shall be kept at all times.

- Labor Law of the People's Republic of China (2018 Amendment)
- Labor Contract Law of the People's Republic of China (2012 Amendment)

I am running a retail business. Can I adopt all the promotion activities and strategies in China as what I did in other countries?

There are quite a number of rules and regulations in relation to business promotion in China, thus it is relatively easy to fall into the pitfall if we are not cautious enough. Excluding a competitor, selling products lower than cost, bundling your products with other products in which the customers may not want to buy, or attracting customers by high-return lottery are all potentially violating the law against unfair competition.

In addition, enterprise would be penalized for compensation if exaggerated and inaccurate advertisement are used. It is advised that all enterprises should understand more about the law before setting out marketing plans for their business.

Case Sharing: Supermarket being penalized for violating Law Against Unfair Competition in a lottery

In 2018, a supermarket run a promotional event of 'annual lottery' to celebrate her anniversary. The supermarket is under promotional event to celebrate its anniversary at its store with an 'annual lucky draw event'. The event stipulates that during the event, members are not required to consume or purchase any products to receive the 'lottery ticket' by presenting the membership card only. The first prize of such lucky draw was a high-definition LCD TV worth RMB 5,900 which exceeds the amount of RMB 5,000. At such, the supermarket has violated the provisions of Anti-Unfair Competition Law of the People's Republic of China that the maximum amount of prize-winning prizes must not exceed 5,000RMB which causes unfair competition behavior resulting in penalties by government authority.

Case Sharing: Sale and Purchase Agreement dispute between Wang and Automobile Sales Company

In 2010, Wang ordered a Volkswagen Sagitar 1.4TSI car in an Automobile Sales Company, who agreed to the price and paid the deposit. However, Wang discovered that the purchased vehicle had been equipped with an additional navigation device with an imported foot pad on collection of car. Wang was also requested to pay the extra fees incurred or else the car could not be picked up.

Wang failed to reach a settlement upon negotiation with the Automobile Sales Company. In order to pick up the car, Wang paid the incurred additional fees for navigation device and imported foot pad unwillingly. Wang then filed the case to court, and court held that the Automobile Sales Company added the navigation device and imported foot pad on the ordered vehicle without the prior consent of Wang, at such, it deprived the decision rights of Wang. The court further held that Wang's act of paying the incurred corresponding consideration is not the true intention of Wang, the sales company shall not install the navigation device and the imported foot pad on the vehicle without the consent of Wang. The court decided the Automobile Sales Company trading behavior shall be revoked and order the Company to compensate Wang as well as restoring the vehicle to the specification of what Wang has ordered.

- Anti-Unfair Competition Law of the People's Republic of China (2017 Revision)
- Advertising Law of the People's Republic of China (2015 Revision)
- Eight Model Cases involving Procuratorial Organs' Cracking down on Crimes Infringing on Consumers' Rights and Interests Published by the Supreme People's Procuratorate (2019)
- Law of the People's Republic of China on the Protection of Consumer Rights and Interests (2013 Amendment)

How shall the liability be shared between employer and employee if accidents happen on employees hired by Foreign-invested Enterprise during office hour?

Below are some of the common accidents that may occur during work:

- A traffic accident occurred when an employee of a Chinese Enterprise is on the way to work. Is the enterprise liable and be responsible?

According to the Regulation on Work-Related Injury Insurances, any traffic accidents which are not caused mainly by employee's responsibility or happened in urban transit traffic, ferries, railway trains are defined as work-related injury and the enterprise shall be liable.

- An employee of a Chinese Enterprise is drunk during work and causing physical injury as a result of mistakenly operating the machine. Who should be liable?

According to the regulation on work-related injuries and insurances, any injuries caused by drunken employees are not considered to be work-related injuries.

- Injuries happened to workers of an outsource contractor during the renovation work for the offices of a Chinese Enterprise, who should be liable?

If the workers are directly hired by the Chinese Enterprise to do the renovation work, then the relation between the enterprise and the worker is an employment relation. In such situation, if the worker is injured, the enterprise will be liable and are required to pay the compensation. If the enterprise opts for renovation work contractor with relevant qualifications for renovation work or contractor team with similar qualifications, the relation between the contractor and the enterprise is a contractor relation. In such situation, if any workers are injured during the renovation work, the liability should go to the contractor.

Case Sharing: Which entity should be liable for Mr. Fang's compensation?

Mr. Fang is a worker from the western area of China. In June 2013, Fang had an accident during his work where his left thumb was injured when he was employed by a Foreign-invested Enterprise for part-time work. The work of Fang was assigned by a contractor who was appointed by the Foreign-invested Enterprise. After the accident, the contractor had paid RMB 8,000 as compensation to

Fang for his medical expenses. Fang's thumb had been kept after operation, yet the thumb cannot function as it previously did.

During Fang's stay in the hospital for treatment, he has reached out the contractor (the construction site) as well as the Foreign-invested Enterprise for further compensation on medical expenses and compensation for his living yet he was being rejected. According to the Foreign-invested Enterprise, Fang's accident happened when he carried out the part-time job assigned by the contractor and thus the contractor should be liable for the compensation. As Fang did not sign any contract with either the contractor or the Foreign-invested Enterprise, Fang was unable to locate who should be responsible for his compensation. However, in this case, since the contractor hired by the Foreign-invested Enterprise is not a licensed and qualified contractor, the liability went to the Foreign-invested Enterprise. On the other hand, if the Foreign-invested Enterprise appointed a proper licensed contractor which has the capability to carry out its work on behalf of its own entity, the contractor shall solely be liable for Fang for his compensation.

■ Regulation on Work-Related Injury Insurance (2010 Revision)

What are the major areas of concerns for Foreign Enterprises to sign cooperation agreements with Chinese entities?

Contract is a big topic. The contents of the contract shall be negotiated and agreed by the parties entering the contract. A common cooperation contracts shall include: (1) the parties; (2) the subject matter; (3) the quantity; (4) the quality; (5) the price; (6) the time limit, place and manner of performance; (7) payment methods; (8) liability for breach of contract; (9) ways to resolve disputes. The content of the contract must be clear and unambiguous, and the terms of the contract should comply with the relevant laws and regulations.

Below are some points to note which can be easily overlooked:

- The parties, including their names and residential address, must be included in every contract. Identifying the contracting party is the first key element of a binding and enforceable contract. Identities of the contracting parties are the most important part of a contract. All the contracting parties mentioned in the contract must be clear enough to be identified with the names, and residential addresses of the contracting parties shall be included in the contract. If there is any ambiguity in relation to the contracting parties, it may affect the validity of the contract in which it will be difficult in identifying the rights and responsibilities of all the concerned parties in the contract. In case of disputes arise and when the contract involves multiple but unclear identity parties, it will increase the difficulty to resolve the dispute.
- The capacity of the contracting parties will affect the nature of

the contract. For instance, is this a civil contract or administrative contract? The contracting party must have the capacity to enter into the contract or else the validity of the contract will be affected. In addition, in the signature column on the last page of the contract, the Chinese Enterprise responsible for signing must be the legal representative of the entity or an authorized legal representative, signature must be in black ink or roller pen (not ball pen). The seal for contract must be the company's official seal or registered specific seal for contract. The contract should be covered with a sewing seal and printed in duplicate for both contracting parties to retain the original. If the contract is signed by non-statutory legal representative of the enterprise, the validity of the contract may be uncertain.

- Default Liability. Default Liability refers to the legal liability arise when one or more of the contracting party or both contracting parties fail to fulfil an obligation or only partly fulfil an obligation. The purpose for default liability is to make sure the contracting parties fulfil the obligation of the agreed contract in order to avoid or compensate loss of the contracting parties. It is a crucial term to guarantee the contract is properly enforced. According to Contract Law and relevant regulations, there are several remedies to avoid the contracting parties from default in fulfilling the contracting terms. However, it is still a usual practice to include default liability in a proper contract to protect the contracting parties, ensuring smooth execution of the contracting terms and effective solutions to resolve disputes. Such remedies for default liabilities include deposits, default compensation, late or specific compensation with interest.
- Dispute resolution method refers to the agreed ways to resolve disputes. In general, negotiation, mediation, arbitration and litigation are the common means for the disputing parties to reach settlement. If the disputing parties opt for designated dispute resolution method in the contract, it will greatly decrease the cost

when disputes arise. According to arbitration regulation, if arbitration is the dispute resolution that the contracting parties agree to adopt, the clause must be explicit and clear. Such clause will exclude the court from jurisdiction over the disputes with a benefit of convenience and efficiency in cross-border contract enforcement when it involves two or more jurisdictions of the contracting parties. (China is one of the members of New York Convention)

- Whenever a Foreign Enterprise enters a contract with a Chinese Enterprise, it should pay special attention to the content of the contract and beware of the national regulations and restrictions or the contract can be invalid or void even after it is properly signed by both parties. For instance, some of the activities or subject matters such as unidentified and unapproved cross-border loan, security agreements or high-risk industries may still be prohibited to foreign investment.

Case Sharing: Police arrest a man for fraud with unapproved seal of a foreign commercial bank

In August 2012, Hongkou police successfully cracked down a contract fraud case in relation to fraudulently collecting fund under the name of a foreign bank. In July 2012, Ms. Huang reported to the police of Hongkou that Liang had recommended a financial product of a foreign commercial bank to her. Liang claimed that the financial product is designed for VIP clients to celebrate the newly established foreign commercial bank in China. The product offers a return of 5% in 28 days. For clients who can invested over RMB 100,000 can enjoy a set of iPhone and RMB 500 coupon cash as immediate reward. Huang had questioned Liang about the reliability of the financial product that Liang recommended and

Liang replied by showing the Financial Investment Agreement of the bank with official seal of the commercial bank. Huang believed in Liang after seeing the contract, and since they were acquainted for years, she agreed to pay RMB 200,000 to Liang.

After 28 days as agreed, Huang called Liang to inquire about the return of the financial product. However, Liang could not be reached, and Huang went to the bank for further enquiries. The bank replied that Liang is not the staff of the bank and the business of the bank is not yet started. At that moment, Huang realized that she was being deceived and reported to the police to file the case. Police of Hongkou acted promptly and started the investigation immediately. In less than a month time, police was able to locate and arrested Liang. After Liang was arrested, he admitted that he took advantage of Huang's curiosity in financial product of foreign commercial bank and deceive her by pretending to be the staff of the commercial bank with a fake 'official seal' of the bank engraved by himself without the permission of the bank.

- Contract Law of the People's Republic of China, 1999

Can Chinese entity and Foreign Enterprise decide the jurisdiction of their contracts?

In general, Chinese enterprises would prefer local jurisdiction when it enters into an agreement with foreign entities. And vice versa, the foreign entities would prefer the agreement to be governed under a foreign jurisdiction of where the entities are from. The main logic for such phenomena is driven by the convenience and a better understanding towards each of their own local law when remedies are needed. In case when there is dispute on the jurisdiction of the contract between the two parties on negotiating a contract, sometimes people may suggest a 'relatively neutral' jurisdiction such as 'Hong Kong' or 'Singapore' for easier agreement by both parties. For a foreign-related Chinese contract, Hong Kong is a commonly selected place of jurisdiction. However, two points need to be noted. First, the court in Hong Kong is not obliged to govern all contract just because it has mentioned that the governing jurisdiction as Hong Kong. Hong Kong courts will accept a case based on the principle of material control, that is, a case requires to have a close connection with Hong Kong, such as either the contract signing place, place of performance, plaintiff, defendant, or property located are in Hong Kong. If there is no such connection point as above, the Hong Kong court will not accept the case. Hong Kong courts would only accept cases with elements closely related to Hong Kong. On the other side, arbitration organizations normally do not have a material connection requirement for accepting a case.

Second, if the foreign-related contracts are related to specific industry or specific governing areas such as land-related, labor-related, Sino-foreign joint venture related, the law applies and the governing jurisdiction could not be agreed by the parties freely.

Case Sharing: Mainland China and Hong Kong agree upon bilateral arrangement regarding interim measures for Arbitration

In 2019, Mainland China and Hong Kong have announced a bilateral arrangement by which the Chinese courts recognize and enforce interim measures in support of institutional arbitration seated in Hong Kong. This is an agreement allowing interim protection for assets, evidence, and other measures in mainland China involved in arbitration cases heard in Hong Kong.

The PRC courts have historically been unwilling to award such measures in support of arbitrations seated outside of Mainland China, the arrangement will further enhance Hong Kong's attractiveness as a seat for China-related international arbitrations. Parties may now conduct 'offshore' arbitration in Hong Kong whilst keeping open the potential for interim measures in Mainland China.

Reader shall further note that Hong Kong and Mainland China have entered into reciprocal arrangements with respect to the enforcement of arbitral awards and court judgments, signed in 2000 and 2019 respectively.

- The Civil Procedure Law of the People's Republic of China (2017 Revision)
- Contract Law of the People's Republic of China, 1999

My foreign company has a sales and purchase agreement with a Chinese entity. We receive the rumors that the Chinese company is to be closed soon when we are about to deliver our goods, what can we do?

There are three kinds of defense right under the Chinese contract law, namely, the defense right for simultaneous performance, defense right of plea against the advance performance, and uneasy defense right.

- Defence right for simultaneous performance: The contracting parties has owed debt to each other and there is no defined sequence in fulfilling the obligation. Obligations of the contracting parties shall be fulfilled simultaneously at the same time. Either party can terminate the contract before the other party perform the obligation. If one party fail to perform according to the contract, the other party has the right to withhold performance.
- Counterargument right of plea against the advance performance: The contracting parties owe each other debts. There is a sequence for the parties to perform the debts and liabilities. In case the first in order fail to perform, the other party can have the right to withhold performance.
- 'Uneasy' Defense Right: The performing party for debt can terminate the contract and withhold performance if there is evidence of the following situations: 1. The other party encounters business downturn; 2. The other party intended to transfer the money away to avoid the debt; 3.Loss of business reputation; 4.

Loss of capability to perform duty to pay the debt. If either party does not have any evidence of any these situations and withhold performance, it is regarded as breach of contract. If the parties suspend performance in accordance with the provisions of Contract Law, they shall promptly notify the other party. When the other party provides appropriate guarantees, one shall resume performance. After the suspension of performance, if the other party fails to resume performance within a reasonable period of time and fails to provide appropriate guarantees, the party that suspends the performance may terminate the contract.

According to the actual situation of the case, foreign suppliers may consider starting relevant legal procedures to claim their right of defense against contract performance and suspend delivery of goods to protect its own legitimate rights and interests.

■ Contract Law of the People's Republic of China, 1999

There are two different terms about deposits when entering a China-relate contract, which terminology is better and what are their differences?

According to the Chinese contract law, the terminology 'payment in advance' and 'deposits' are usually seen in contracts. People get easily mix them up because the two terminology carries different meaning. So, which one is better or more appropriate? It all depends whether you are buyer or seller and the expectation when you enter a contract.

'Payment in advance' refers to a wish to buy, if the other party does not perform as agreed, the 'Advance payment' will be returned to the buyer whereas a 'Deposit' refers to a promise or a guarantee. If the other party cannot perform as promised, the deposit will not be returned or refunded, and a compensation will be resulted due to the failure of performance. For seller, if deposits are received but performance is withheld, seller must compensate the buyer with two times of the deposits paid. Here are the basic rules related to the operation of deposit:

- The parties may agree that one party shall pay the deposit to the other party as a guarantee for the creditor's rights. After the debtor has performed the debt, the deposit shall be refunded or recovered. If the party paying the deposit fails to perform the agreed debt, it has no right to request a refund of the deposit; if the party receiving the deposit fails to perform the agreed debt, it shall return two times the deposit.
- The deposit shall be agreed in writing. The parties shall agree on the time limit for the payment of the deposit in the deposit contract. The deposit contract shall take effect from the date of actual delivery of the deposit and the actual paid sum.
- The amount of the deposit shall be agreed upon by the parties but shall not exceed 20% of the amount of the main contract.

Case Sharing: Who shall keep the deposits in the 'Subscription Agreement'?

Liang and Wei planned to get married by the end of 2017 and planned to purchase a property. On 1 May 2016, Liang and Wei signed a 'Subscription Agreement' at a local real estate agency and paid RMB 20,000 as deposit. According to Liang and Wei, prior to signing of the 'Subscription Agreement', the sales inform that the property can be transferred to Liang and Wei by 31 Dec 2016. Yet, Liang and Wei realized that the property can only be transferred to them on 31 Dec 2017 after payment was made. Since the date was later than expectation required for their marriage, Liang and Wei requested the sales department of the Real Estate Agent to refund the deposit of RMB 20,000 but were being rejected. The Court held that the payment made to the Real Estate Agency is a deposit by nature and it should be compensated to the party dependent upon the fault and breach of contract of either party. However, according to the evidence, it is hard to confirm that the seller promised the date for transferring of property is 31 Dec 2016 when the agreement is entered. The two contracting parties cannot reach a settlement, and due to insufficient evidence demonstrating one party has breached the contract, the Court held that the Real Estate Agency shall return Liang and Wei RMB 20,000 (the original deposit sum) instead of returning two times the deposit.

■ The Guarantee Law of the People's Republic of China,1995

Products of our company have been counterfeited in China. What can I do?

The trademark registration and protection system in China is independent from other countries and areas (including Hong Kong). Therefore, you should register your trademarks in China disregarding what you have did in other places. If a trademark is registered only in a foreign country, the trademark will not be automatically protected in the China, and vice versa.

There are various common types of counterfeiting behaviors depend on the specific circumstances. It may constitute acts of unfair competition or may be an infringement of relevant intellectual property protection laws, including trademark rights, patent rights, copyrights and trade secrets.

According to the Anti-Unfair Competition Law, the departments that supervise and perform regular inspection of unfair competition behaviors in China are mainly the administrative departments for industry and commerce. In addition, it also includes other departments with power to conduct supervision and inspection as stipulated by laws and administrative regulations. For example, the Ministry of Domestic Trade and the Ministry of Foreign Trade and Economic Cooperation have the right to supervise unfair competition in domestic trade and foreign trade; the State Bureau of Technical Supervision has the power to supervise unfair competition in relation to quality; The Patent office and the State Administration of Press, Publications, Radio, Film and Television of the People's Republic of China has the power to supervise unfair competition in relation to the patent and publishing industry; the Ministry of Supervision, the Ministry of Public Security, the Ministry of Construction, the Ministry of Chemical Industry, the Ministry of Culture, and other ministries and commissions also have the right to unfair competition in relation to their functions and industries, and etc.

When an infringement occurs, the right holder or interested party may request the corresponding administrative authorities to handle it or may file a civil lawsuit directly with the local court. The types of administrative penalties include fines, orders to stop violations, confiscation of illegal earning, and confiscation of infringing products. Where the circumstances of intellectual property infringement are serious, the person directly responsible shall be investigated for criminal responsibility according to law.

Case Sharing: WING WAH - A trademark dispute that costed client 10 million legal fee

Bitter dispute over Wing Wah mooncake brand back in court. Hong Kong Catering Group Wing Wah (Wing Wah) was in court against Guangdong Foshan Shunde Sushi Ronghua Food Co., Ltd. and Zhongshan Jiming Food Co., Ltd (Su) for the battle over the use of its brand name and the product design. It dated back to 1999 when Hong Kong Wing Wah mooncake discovered Su has produced similar products using its trademarks and packaging design. Wing Wah and Su had started civil proceedings in local court.

Hong Kong Wing Wah sued Su for securing the right to use the trademarks in China and acquired the rounded logo of Wing Wah written in simplified Chinese characters. On the other hand, Su believed that it should enjoy the trademark rights granted by the Chinese government according the law of People's Republic of China based on first-come-first-register principle. The key point of arguments of the series of cases lie on the viewpoint of Hong Kong Wing Wah that it belongs to 'renowned (well-known) brand'.

The People's Court finally ruled that Su had infringed the rights of Wing Wah and ordered Su to stop all the infringement by ceasing the use of the packaging. The two had involved in length court cases, according to records related, disputes between the two suing each other was over 58 cases, involving litigation fee over RMB 10 million.

Most clients may mistakenly overlook the risks of counterfeit when decide to enter the China market without prior preparation and protection plan. In China, the rules for intellectual property right applications are primarily a first-come-first-register basis. In other words, the general rule is whoever register whatever brand first, the applicant for registration owns the intellectual property rights of the brand.

- Anti-Unfair Competition Law of the People's Republic of China (2017 Revision)
- Trademark Law of the People's Republic of China (2019 Amendment)
- Patent Law of the People's Republic of China (2008 Amendment)
- Copyright Law of the People's Republic of China (2010 Amendment)
- Interpretation (II) of the Supreme People's Court on Several Issues concerning the Application of Law in the Trial of Patent Infringement Dispute Cases, 2016
- Ten Model Cases on Intellectual Property Protection by China Customs in 2015 Issued by the General Administration of Customs, 2016

Since the business is not ideal as expected, I intend to cease the operation of the business in China. What should I do?

Companies that intend to cease the operation of its business shall be liquidated and deregistered. The main formality for winding up a company include liquidation, that is, the establishment of the liquidation group to take over the company's management to carry out liquidation work, announcement, notify creditors to declare creditor's rights, propose liquidation plan, allocate surplus property, go to the tax office and relevant authorization to arrange deregistration, closure of bank accounts, and finally go to the industrial and commercial authorities for final deregistration. A liquidation group normally composed of personnel of relevant departments or agencies or a professional institution such as a law firm, an accounting firm or a bankruptcy liquidation firm established according to law.

If the company is dissolved and liquidated according to law, the liquidation group shall, within 10 days from the date of establishment, file the list of the members of the liquidation group and the person in charge of the liquidation group with the company registration authority. The company shall be terminated upon cancellation of registration by the company registration authority.

In case if an enterprise fails to pay off the debts due and the assets are insufficient to pay off all the debts or the apparent lack of liquidity, the debts shall be cleared in accordance to Bankruptcy law; Under specific circumstances, it may also opt for reorganization in accordance to Bankruptcy law. Debtors can file an application for reorganization according to Bankruptcy, and if the debtor is unable to pay off the debt due, the creditor may also apply to the people's court for reorganization or bankruptcy liquidation. If an enterprise has been dissolved but has not been liquidated, and the assets are insufficient to pay off the debts, the person responsible for liquidation according to Bankruptcy law shall apply to the people's court for a bankruptcy liquidation.

If an enterprise does not operate normally or ceases to operate for a prolonged period of time, it will be revoked by the State Administration for Industry and Commerce and cause adverse effects not only just on the company but also on the legal representative and its shareholders. For example, a company that do not submit annual audit report (if required) or pay tax on schedule will be under monitoring and warned by relevant authorities. In case of prolonged abnormal operation of company, not only the company itself will be penalized, the legal representative and shareholder of the said company could be fined and 'blacklisted' by authorities including the Industrial and Commercial Bureau.

- Enterprise Bankruptcy Law of the People's Republic of China, 2006
- China Company Law of the People's Republic of China, revised 2018
- Regulation of the People's Republic of China on the Administration of Company Registration (2016 Revision)

I run business in China under my personal capacity, but I failed and ended with debts. Can I apply for bankruptcy?

Sorry, individuals cannot apply for bankruptcy in China! Enterprise Bankruptcy Law applicable to Company and Partnership but not individuals. (*Note: In July 2019, the National Development and Reform Commission along with 12 other government departments said they would take measures to promote the establishment of a bankruptcy system for insolvent individuals step-by-step.*) Therefore, in case where a natural person cannot pay all the debts by all his personal assets to the creditors, the case can be followed up and enforceable by civil procedures endlessly. In other words, creditor can enforce a court judgment any time when the debtor does not cooperate to pay the debt. Some of the common practices include adding the debtor into the List of Dishonest Persons subject to Enforcement (known as 'Blacklist') and impose credit-related punishment such as imposing restrictions to the investment, working, loans, expenses, living in hotel, travel by airplane or high-speed train and exit restrictions to forbidding the individual to leave the country. Further detail as below.

- If the person fails to perform the obligations determined by the legal documents in accordance with the enforcement notice, the people's court shall have the right to inquire the relevant entities about the deposits, bonds, stocks, fund shares and other property of the executed person. The people's court has the power to retain, freeze, transfer, and change the property of the person subject to execution according to different circumstances.
- If the person fails to perform the obligations set out in the legal documents in accordance with the enforcement notice, the people's court shall have the right to retain and withdraw the income of the part of the person subject to performance of the obligation. However, the necessary expenses for the living of the person being executed and the dependents they support should be retained.
- After the people's court adopts the enforcement measures, if the enforced person is still unable to repay the debt, the obligation should continue until fulfilled. Whenever the creditor discovers that the person has other property, he may apply to the people's court to enforce again at any time.
- If the person fails to perform the obligations determined by the

legal documents, the people's court may notify the relevant government authorities to assist in the adoption of restrictions on exit, record in the credit information system, publish information on non-performance obligations through the media, and other provisions prescribed by law.

- If the person fails to perform the payment obligations in force in the period specified in the execution notice, the people's court may limit his high consumption (which means 'living an expensive life'). Violating the restriction order on high consumption orders is a contempt of court, the person involved shall be detained and fined; serious offence will lead to further criminal liability.

Case Sharing: A traffic accident that result in over RMB 10 million of compensation

In July 2011, a bridge in Huairou District of Beijing was crushed by a large truck weighing over 110 tons. The truck driver Zhang was sentenced to 4 years in prison for committing traffic accidents and compensated the Huairou Highway Branch of the Beijing Municipal Traffic Commission for an economic loss of RMB 15.56 million The driver and the owner (his son) of the vehicle were jointly liable for the compensation. Since individual cannot apply for bankruptcy in China, the debt of RMB 15 million means that Zhang and his son have to carry extremely heavy debts for the rest of their lives.

Up till now, personal bankruptcy is not an option in China, although in this type of exceptional case individual can apply for special relieve from local court, i.e. when the citizen has no income source or encounter loss of ability to work. This is one way to help poor people who are truly incapable of paying debt. According to law, people who is unable to repay the loan due to difficulties in life, has no source of income, and loses the ability to work, the people's court can rule that the execution shall be terminated.

As such, foreigner should pay extra attention, and is always suggested to run business in China under a proper limited liability company.

- The Civil Procedure Law of the People's Republic of China (2017 Revision)
- Several Provisions of the Supreme People's Court on Restricting High Consumption and Relevant Consumption of Persons Subject to Enforcement (2015 Amendment)

PART III Working & Living in China

If I frequently represent my company to work in China, do I need any application?

Increasing numbers of foreigners working or doing in business in China has become a trend. If expatriates only represent their foreign companies for a short-term visit for business purposes such as procurement cooperation or other business-related activities, working visa is generally not required. In case of secondment of a foreign employee of foreign enterprise to China, application for working permit and visa must be applied. Expatriates seek to work for its employer which is a local Chinese company shall obtain the relevant Labor permits issued by Labor Department, otherwise the labor relation or the Labor contract will be invalid if such permits are not applied. The local company will be liable to other relevant breach of regulations.

Foreigners with 'Foreign Expert Certificate' and 'Foreigner's Work Permit' may establish an employment relationship with an employer in China. If a foreigner fails to obtain a valid work permit or visa and entered a labor contract with a Chinese employer, the court will not support the existence of a labor relationship in case of dispute.

- The Provisions on the Employment of Foreigners in China (2010

Amendment)
- Interim Measures for the Participation in Social Insurance of Foreigners Employed in China (2011)
- Interpretation (IV) of the Supreme People's Court of Several Issues on the Application of Law in the Trial of Labor Dispute Cases (2013)

What are the major concerns for expatriate to work in China as employee?

As an employee working in China, an expatriate should be aware of the following:

1. Identify the capacity employing you as employer

Do not take it for granted and overlook the employing capacity which enters into employment contract with you to establish the employment relationship. You may be signing an employment contract with another unknown entity which is not the entity employing you. (May be of two different similar names of the company). Foreigners working in China should only work for and be employed by legally registered entities. For instance, individual economic organization and individuals are not allowed to employ foreigner as employee. In addition, according to law of People's Republic of China, foreign enterprise must start its business activities only when its representative office or branch office in China is operated. If the Chinese company directly hires the foreigner as employee, such employment relation between the Chinese company the foreign employee will not be protected by the Labor Law of People's Republic of China. If there is dispute between the Chinese company and the foreign employee, it would only be regarded as civil matters.

2. Retain the original all the relevant contracts and files

Many of the expatriates working in China would refer to the law of their own domiciles. Some of them are from western countries and may overlook the importance in retaining the originals of documents to be used as evidence and proof. They may neglect the importance and in particular the requirement of Chinese authorities in relation to the format of formal written documents or the requirement of the official seal.

We strongly advise foreigners employed in China to request for the original of documents such as employment contracts and request for documents to be written in both English and Chinese. If the required employment visa and working permit are not applied and if the labor contract is not properly written or sealed, the Labor Arbitration Committee will not accept the application of the case when dispute arises. Moreover, the Committee will not issue the 'Notice for non-acceptance' so that the dispute cannot be handled by People's Court. Lastly, if disputes arise and resulted in litigation or arbitration, the applicant shall prepare and be ready to submit all sorts of written evidence according to the relevant requirements.

3. Properly apply for employment visa as required

To apply for employment visa, the actual employer must be the applicant for application. If there is only labor contract without apply for employment visa, the employment relation shall not be protected by the Labor Law. According to Interpretation (IV) of the Supreme People's Court of Several Issues on the Application of Law in the Trial of Labor Dispute Cases, if a foreigner working in China fails to apply an employment visa according to law, the court will not support the employment relation between the employer and the employee. If the labor contract is considered to be invalid, the Labor Arbitration Committee will issue a Notice of Non-Acceptance for filing case at the People's court depending on the location of operation of the employer. Such lawsuit may not be ruled according to Labor Law but civil-relation law regarding the employment relations. The monetary claims for such case will not be supported by the court.

In addition, foreigners who have not formally apply for their employment shall be subject to termination of employment, fines, and prohibition of exiting and re-entering China according to the Exit-Entry Administration Law of the People's Republic of China. Therefore, if the employee wants to report their employers for illegal employment, the individual will be defined as illegal employee.

4. Understand your rights and obligations

According to National Treatment principle, foreign employees in China shall enjoy the same employment benefits (including enjoying the benefits of social insurance) and responsibilities as Chinese employees. For instance, companies shall not retain the working permit of any individuals and request for claims imposed on employees for loss in terms of property in any format.

- The Provisions on the Employment of Foreigners in China (2010 Amendment)
- Labor Law of the People's Republic of China (2018 Amendment)
- Labor Contract Law of the People's Republic of China (2012

Amendment)

What are the details I should be aware of if I sign employment contract with company in China?

If an expatriate is hired by Chinese company or if the labor contract is signed in China, labor law and regulations of China applies.

When expatriates sign labor contracts in China, they should pay attention to the following:

- Employees should go through the details of the labor contract in terms of major terms and conditions, time limit of the contract, restrictions, probation, job description, working time, wages, overtime pay, social security insurance, allowances for living and the payment method of wages, the IP rights of your work, confidentiality agreement or non-disclosure agreement as well as the liabilities or breaching the labor contract or termination, etc. All of these should be clearly written. Among all, the restrictions and prohibited terms involve more about the rights and responsibilities of the employees which would easily lead to disputes. Employers may abuse its position to impose some unreasonable terms and conditions on the employees and force the employees to accept. For instance, the employer may ask the employees to be responsible for a wider scope of responsibilities in order to avoid the company to be liable for its own liabilities. For probation period, the law of China has clear provisions. For Labor contract with term over three months but less than one year, the probationary period

shall not exceed one month; for Labor contract with term over one year but less than three years, the probationary period shall not exceed two months; for Labor contract with term over three years or no fixed-term Labor contract, the probationary period shall not exceed six months.
- After signing the labor contract, the employer shall apply for working permit for the employee.
- For termination of labor contract, employees may terminate the contract if they realize that the actual employment conditions vary seriously from the conditions as stated in the labor contract or if the employees find themselves unfit for the employment. If the employee wants to terminate the contact, apart during the probationary period, the employee shall notify the employer in writing 30 days in advance with relevant reasons. If the employer wants to terminate the employee, the employer shall refer to the violations of labor disciplines, serious misconduct, cheating at work, crimes or under-performance during probationary period as reasons to terminate the labor contract and go through the required legitimate procedures.
- In case of dispute for termination of labor contract, the parties can negotiate for settlement with the Labor Authorities. If negotiation fails, the case will usually be handled by the Labor Dispute Arbitration Committee.
- Apart from receiving wages, employees working in China shall pay individual salary tax and the social security insurance. All employees should understand the relevant situation before signing of labor contract.

Case Sharing: Hong Kong people's working permit in China expired Labor contract is invalid

In 2005, the plaintiff Ms. Lam joined a bank and was stationed in the defendant's China office and signed a labor contract with the defendant (a China subsidiary of a Hong Kong bank). The contract was for three years and the monthly salary was RMB 43,500. In September 2007, the plaintiff's working permit expired, and both parties did not apply for the extension of the working permit. In December 2007, the plaintiff and the defendant signed another 'labor contract' with a contract term of one year. The basic salary was RMB 19,000 per month plus bonus. As of December 2008, the defendant issued a Notice of Termination of Labor Contract to the plaintiff on the grounds of the expiration of the labor contract, and the plaintiff signed the notice on the same day.

The plaintiff reflected that at the end of 2007, the defendant proposed to lower the plaintiff's wages, but at the same time ensured that the plaintiff's annual income after taxation could reach RMB 400,000 by issuing the year-end bonus, and the plaintiff was required to re-sign the contract. The plaintiff accepted the defendant's request based on personal trust. However, in the end the defendant did not pay the year-end bonus and related expenses as promised, and the two parties had a labor dispute as such.

After the court hearing, it was ruled that the plaintiff Ms. Lam's validity period for the 'Taiwan, Hong Kong and Macao Personnel Working Permit' had expired when the plaintiff signed the last labor contract with the defendant, and the working permit was not renewed. The labor contract in dispute between the employer and the employee was invalid and was not protected by the Labor Law of China. Yet the employee did work for the employer, the employer shall comply with the labor contract to pay the relevant wages and bonus. However, regarding the year-end bonus as mentioned in the labor contract, it shall be paid on discretion according to the actual performance of the company and the employer has the right to determine the amount without leading to violation of law. And for the economic compensation and extra compensation for the plaintiff, the defendant shall not pay according to the invalid labor contract.

To conclude, the court is not considering an employment relationship to have been established when an expatriate enters into a labor contract with his supposedly employer if the expatriate fails to process for and obtain the relevant work permit.

- Labor Contract Law of the People's Republic of China (2012 Amendment)
- Provisions on the Employment of Foreigners in China (2010 Amendment)
- Interpretation (IV) of the Supreme People's Court of Several Issues on the Application of Law in the Trial of Labor Dispute Cases (2013)

My Chinese colleagues have joined the social security insurance scheme, do I need one too?

China's social security system comprises of five different types of insurance and one mandatory housing fund. The five insurances are pension, medical, work-related injury, unemployment, and maternity insurances. This is commonly known as the saying of 'five insurance and one fund' in China:

- Endowment insurance is the most important among the 'five insurance'. It is mandatory and compulsory in order to protect the living of employees after they are retired. Both employers and employees must participate in the 'five insurance and one fund' scheme. Companies are required to report on a monthly basis. Premiums vary from region to region. Employees are required to make monthly payment equivalent to 8% of their wages (with a maximum amount) and corporate contributions at 10%.

- Medical insurance is also under the mandatory national security system. When an employee is sick or injured, the medical insurance will help the employee to receive immediate medication treatment or economic compensation to reduce the medical risk caused by sickness or injury. Taking Shenzhen as example, the contribution is calculated based on 0.8% to 1% of wages of the employees and paid by the employer.
- Unemployment insurance is also mandatory through legislation with the purpose of providing assistance to employees while they are unemployed. Employers shall pay the premium of the unemployment insurance based on 0.4% of the wages of the employees. Employees are not required to pay any premium.
- The purpose of work injury insurance is to prevent and to share the risks of occupational injury. It shall be paid by employer and employees are not required to pay.
- The housing provident fund is the long-term savings for both employers and employees in relation to housing benefit. All the residents of cities and provinces shall pay such premium. The minimum deposit ratio for employees and employers on housing provident funds is 5% each, with a maximum ratio of 12%.

According to law, foreigners who are lawfully recruited and employed by enterprises, public institutions, social organizations, privately-run non-enterprise entities, foundations, law firms, accounting firms and other organizations duly registered within the territory of China shall participate in the basic endowment (old-age) insurance for employees, basic medical insurance for employees, work injury insurance, unemployment insurance and maternity insurance in accordance with the law, with the employers and the persons in question paying social insurance contributions as prescribed.

The employer who hires foreigners shall process social insurance registration for the foreigners recruited and employed within 30 days from the date of its processing their working permits.

Therefore, after expatriates working in China have signed employment contracts with Chinese Enterprises, they are also required to take part in relevant social security insurance. Employers in China must purchase social security insurance for their employees.

For a foreigner who leaves China before reaching the statutory pension age, the social insurance individual account shall be retained, and shall be renewed on a cumulative basis when the person returns to work in China. Alternatively, upon written application for closing the social insurance account from the person, the balance in the individual account can be returned in lump-sum to the said person. The balance in the social insurance individual account of a deceased foreigner may be inherited pursuant to the law.

It is good to note that, China has signed social security agreements with a dozen of countries, but so far not all of them have been fully implemented. At the moment, expatriates from Germany, South Korea, Denmark, Canada, Finland, Switzerland, the Netherlands, Spain, Luxembourg, and Japan are more likely eligible for some degree of social security exemptions in China. Since labor relation and social insurance are managed at a regional level, we expect some variations may exist among cities.

Case Sharing: Foreign Company hiring Chinese employees directly without social security insurance is liable to pay medical fees as compensation

In October 2010, a representative office of a foreign company in Guangzhou directly hired a Chinese employee Wang and signed a labor contract with Wang. When Wang commenced her work, the representative office did go to the social security bureau to pay the social security insurance for Wang. However, the social security bureau rejected the request of the representative office to pay social security insurance under the name of representative office. Therefore, Wang had been working for the representative office without social security insurance acquired.

In March 2011, Wang was diagnosed with cancer and paid RMB 300,000 for her medical treatment expenses. Wang claimed her medical expenses with the representative office after she had left the hospital. The representative office refused to pay Wang and did not agree to the responsibility of paying medical fee for Wang especially when the representative office had attempted to pay the social security insurance for Wang but got rejected. Wang failed to negotiate with the representative office and filed the case to the court.

The court held that the representative office should be responsible for the medical expenses for Wang despite it did not acquire the social security insurance for Wang. According to the authors, the representative office in this case may not be aware of its position in acquiring the social security insurance. According to law of China, representative office is not legally positioned to directly hire Chinese employees or sign labor contract with its employees. Yet, representative office is legitimate to hire Chinese employees through licensed recruitment agents and acquire the social security insurance for its employees. In the judgment of this case, the court ruled that the representative office had not entered a proper employment relation with Wang through the foreign-related employment bureau so that Wang's medical expenses could not be compensated through the social security insurance. Therefore, the representative office should be responsible to pay Wang the medical fees supposed to be paid by the insurance fund.

- Interim Measures for the Participation in Social Insurance of Foreigners Employed in China, 2011
- Social Insurance Law of the People's Republic of China (2018 Amendment)

How shall I pay tax if I always live in foreign countries but employed in China?

Whether or not an individual shall pay salary tax to Chinese Tax Authorities depends on multiple factors including the relevant sources of income, payment method of the income, and period of time residing in China. For details, please refer to the 'Regulation on the Implementation of the Individual Income Tax Law of the People's Republic of China, as amended 2018' and the tax reform staring 2019 between the two places. The general principles are as follows:

- If a foreign resident working in China for a prolong period of time with self-owned property in China, the resident has already fallen within the requirement to pay tax to Chinese Tax Authorities according to the Individual Income Tax Law of the People's Republic of China and the definition 'is domiciled in China'. For the purpose of the Individual Income Tax Law, 'is domiciled in China' means habitually residing inside China due to household registration, family or economic ties; and 'income obtained inside and outside China' means income derived from inside and outside China respectively. Such person must pay tax to China Tax Authorities according to the income earned in China and also the income earned outside China including income from elsewhere in the world.
- A person who lives in China for consecutive 5 years or over 1 year starting from the sixth year shall file a tax assessment for the income earned in China and outside China. If the person does not live for 1 year in China, the person shall only pay tax according the income earned in China.
- Individuals who do not have a residence in China but have been living in China for 1 year (or 183 days) and not more than 5 years, their wages paid by either Chinese company or foreign company earned in China shall be considered taxable income.
- Expatriates who do not have a permanent residence in China but have been living in China for 1 year and not more than 5 years are obliged to pay taxes. Expatriates staying in China for less than 1 year with work remuneration earned in China shall pay income tax.
- Expatriates work and stay in China for less than 183 days (time limit of the tax treaty), the taxable income will only be

calculated based on the income earned in China. The actual taxable payment amount will be calculated based on the number of days staying in China.

For expatriate travelling to and from two countries frequently, they may involve income from both places and resulted in double taxation. First of all, depending on the tax arrangement and regulations (if any) between China and the country of nationality of the expatriate, if the individual income tax has been paid in China, he or she may apply for deduction of the tax in his / her own country by submitting relevant supporting documents such as tax payment receipt. For more information on avoiding double taxation, please consult a professional or the relevant tax authority.

The individual income tax of employees working in China is generally paid by the company reflecting on the actual wages paid to the employees. The relevant company must pay taxes and submit tax returns to the local tax authorities within the specified time limit. Generally, the individual income tax in China is subject to a progressive tax rate ranging from 5% to 45%. According to reference materials of year 2014, foreigners with monthly income exceeding RMB 4,800 shall pay tax. The tax rate for income over RMB 80,000 is 45%.

Foreign individuals who are liable to pay PRC tax sometimes are required to register with the local tax authorities for providing documents including photocopy of passport, work permit, expert certificate, working contract, house-renting contract and so on. It is worth to note that the following types of income by foreign individuals can enjoy exemption:

- Income from interest, dividends and bonuses from enterprises with foreign investments in China.

- Dividends and bonuses from the share issuing enterprises in China for B or H shareholders.
- Subsidiaries, including housing meal and laundry expenses, relocation and moving expenses, business travel allowances, home leave expenses, language training expenses and children education costs.

■ Individual Income Tax Law of the People's Republic of China (2018 Amendment)

If I work and live frequently in China, am I eligible to apply Chinese Nationality?

Foreign nationals who meet the pre-requisite requirements and conditions are eligible to apply for Chinese Nationality.

According to law, foreigners who meet relevant conditions can apply to become Chinese citizens.

Foreign nationals or persons without a nationality who are willing to abide by China's Constitution and laws and who meet one of the following conditions may be naturalized upon approval of their applications:

- they are near relatives of Chinese nationals, that is, if one is ABC, BBC or have a close national relative;

- they have settled in China, that is, if one has lived in China for an extended period of time; or
- they have other legitimate reasons, these broadly refer to people in senior positions or invested large sums of money in China.

As foreign national, applying for Chinese Nationality may be one of the biggest challenges as to compare with applying for other nationality elsewhere in the world. The People's Republic of China does not recognize dual nationality for any Chinese national. Chinese Nationality applicants are therefore required to renounce other nationalities, if any, upon application in which they may encounter more hurdles than they imagine.

Indeed, one may find quite a number of constraints upon the PRC policies for foreign nationals to immigrate to China. Yet, foreign nationals are very welcomed to reside in China by means of various talents and professional's schemes, including the introduction of policies to grant permanent residency in numerous cities in China to facilitate foreign nationals living in China. In practice, the number of applications for Chinese nationality or residence in major cities such as Beijing are more and the guidelines as well as the application procedures are more standardized. In remote cities or region in China, the procedure to obtaining a Chinese Nationality or residency would be more difficult.

Expatriate can gain his Foreigner's Certificate for Permanent Residence in the PRC (i.e., Chinese green card). Below are some examples of qualifier:

- one who hold a relatively high-level post in China

- one has direct and stable investment in China
- one has made some important contributions to China or be a kind of professionals that China needs
- one is a spouse or unmarried child under 18 of the ones that meet at least one of the 3 above requirements
- one is a spouse of a Chinese citizen
- one is an unmarried child under 18 whose parents are Chinese citizens
- one is over 60 years old and have direct relatives in China and none outside China

And has no criminal records, of course.

For the sake of convenience, foreign nationals may consider the application as Hong Kong Permanent Resident of Hong Kong Special Administrative Region to enjoy the privileges of Hong Kong Permanent Resident working and living in China.

- ■ Nationality Law of the People's Republic of China, 1980

I work frequently in Shenzhen with a stable place of residence in China, shall I apply the resident permit?

First, please note that a resident permit is not the same as a permanent residence (application). Foreigners living in China shall apply a resident permit at the Public Security Authorities based on the requirements for foreign population. The period of residence shall be registered in accordance with the entry visa conditions.

The Exit-Entry Administration Law states that where foreigners stay in hotels in China, the hotels shall register their accommodation in accordance with the regulations on the public security administration of the hotel industry and submit foreigners' accommodation registration information to the public security organs in the places where the hotels are located.

For foreigners who reside or stay in domiciles other than hotels, they or the persons who accommodate them shall, within 24 hours after the foreigners' arrival, go through the registration formalities with the public security organs in the places of residence.

According to law, under the following circumstances, a foreigner maybe fined for up to RMB 2,000:

- Refuse to accept examination of their exit/entry documents by public security organs;
- Refuse to submit their residence permits for examination;
- Fail to go through the formalities for altering registration in accordance with the relevant regulations when there is any change in the registered items in their residence permits;
- Use others' exit/entry documents.

Hotels that fail to process accommodation registration for foreigners shall be punished in accordance with the relevant provisions of the Law of the People's Republic of China on Penalties for Administration of Public Security; hotels that fail to submit foreigners' accommodation registration information to public security organs shall be given a warning; where circumstances are serious, such hotels shall be fined not less than RMB 1,000 but not more than RMB 5,000.

- Exit and Entry Administration of the People's Republic of China, 2012

What are the major areas of concerns if I rent a place of residence in China?

If you need to rent a place of residence in China, you should require the 'Proof of Property Right' (i.e. Real Estate Ownership Certificates or 'The Red Booklet') from the Landlord to verify the details of the Landlord, ensuring you are signing the contract with the right person. Therefore, when renting property as a foreigner, hiring a real estate agent is inevitable.

In case where the contract is set out between the attorney or authorized person for the Landlord, you should request for a proper and valid document to prove authorization and avoid 'housing scams'. Most of these contracts are in Chinese. Expatriates shall request to see an English translation from a certified source, and it is important for you to understand all the terms and conditions of your rental contract.

For signing a proper rental contract, signatures with fingerprints of both Landlord and Tenant are required along with the signed copies of valid identity cards of both parties. According to (Shenzhen City) Housing Leasing Implements Leasing Permit System, signed contracts shall be presented to relevant organization within 10 days after the contract is signed to complete the registration.

The rental contract shall include details concerning the monthly rent, terms of payment, the length of the lease, the amount of the deposit (normally 2 months), restrictions, condition for early termination and services included in the rent. Please also check if you are allowed to keep pets in the apartment.

Illegal acquisitions of properties with Real Estate Ownership Certificates are forbidden from registration of rental contracts. Village buildings can be rented, and registration is required.

Meanwhile, tenants shall ensure the rented property is clean without collaterals. In case if the rented property is mortgaged, the rental relationship shall not be affected. If the property is mortgaged before renting out, there is a risk for the tenant if the creditor exercises its rights upon the collateral, the tenant may be forced to leave the premise and resulted in economic loss. The Landlord should have told the tenant if the property is mortgaged renting to the tenant. In case that the landlord does not inform the tenant about the mortgage arrangement, the landlord is liable for damages.

Case Sharing: Miss Li was deceived in rental matter, staying in the rented property for only two months after paying rental fee for a year

On Feb 2014, Miss Li intended to rent a property in Rong Feng Community by searching the available apartments from relevant websites. During the site visit of the targeted rental apartment, Miss Zhang who claimed to be the spouse of the landlord showed her valid identity card to Miss Li. Miss Zhang further showed the copy of identity card of the Landlord along with copies of the Real

Estate Certificate. Miss Li verified all the documents with relevant organization to confirm the validity and authentication of the documents. Miss Li then decided to rent the target property with Miss Zhang. Miss Zhang suggested Miss Li to pay the rent for 1 year in order to enjoy RMB 100 less for the monthly rental fee, which was RMB 1,200 in total. Miss Li agreed.

Two months later, another property agent contacted Miss Li and requested her to pay the outstanding rent for the next quarter. According to the property agent, the record showed that the tenant of her apartment was Miss Zhang. The landlord of her rented property residing in foreign country had authorized the property agent to collect rental fees. At that point, Miss Li had found that she was unable to contact Miss Zhang. Miss Li reported to the police. The police confirmed that the identity of Miss Zhang was authentic and suggested Miss Li to handle the matter as civil matter (economic dispute). Yet, Miss Li was unable to contact Miss Zhang then.

- General Provisions of the Civil Law of the People's Republic of China, 2017
- Contract Law of the People's Republic of China, 1999
- Shenzhen Special Economic Zone Housing Leasing Regulations, 2004

What should I pay attention to if I drive in China?

In mainland China, traffic aligns on the right-hand side of the road, while people drive on the left in Hong Kong and Macau.

In China, Individual cannot drive with an International Driving

Permit (IDP) nor with the driving permits obtained in Hong Kong, Macau or Taiwan. For people traveling to China for a short period of time, including tourists, they can get a temporary driver's permit for a maximum of three months without needing to pass an exam (although it is not recommended by authors if you do not read Chinese). Normally, you can obtain this at the local traffic police department in the city you are in. In Beijing and possibly in other large cities, it can be obtained directly in the airport.

Expatriates who wants to apply for driving license in China must meet certain requirements. First, the applicant must be residing, working or studying in China for a period of time. Second, the validity of the visa or permit that the foreign national is holding must be over 3 months or above.

Expatriates applying for driving license must complete the application procedures at the authorities at the place of residence, if one acquired a valid driving license in foreign country or district, in most cases the majority of the examination requirement will be exempted (except a multiple-choice examination). Other requirements for application of driving license include the age limitations and physical conditions. Applicants must be over 18 years old and under 70-year-old as well as fit and proper for driving.

To apply driving license in China, expatriates who is the holder of driving license issued by a foreign country shall submit passport, proof of residence, driving license issued in foreign country or international driving license, health check record and exam record of driving test. Road test is not required.

About owning a private car, many cities in China had imposed vehicle restriction policies. Beijing is the first city to allocate vehicle license plates using a lottery system for vehicle purchase.

Applicants for lottery from Hong Kong, Macau or Taiwan or foreign countries with valid ID of China need to live in Beijing for over 1 year to satisfy the requirement.

For non-Beijing residents who reside in Beijing, they are restricted from purchasing vehicles if they neither possess any temporary visa, work visa nor pay Social Security Insurance for 5 consecutive years.

Acquiring vehicle insurance is the first step to take before you can drive in China. There are two types of insurance, namely Statutory General Insurance and Commercial Insurance. Statutory Insurance is strictly required by the Authority and it is compulsory, such insurance offers upper limits on the sum assured for the life of third-party life with death protection. Therefore, you are advised to acquire another commercial insurance with better coverage and higher sum assured. The amount of sum assured is suggested to be adequate for the compensation for the third party upon accident arises. If accident happens, apart from paying the compensation for death benefit for the third party, the responsible party shall also pay the relevant medical fee, benefit in lieu of wages, hospital fee (including admission fee and in-patient meals), nursing fees, ancillary relief for disability, funeral fee, dependent living expenses, compensation for the psychological harm for next of kin of the victims.

According the relevant rules and regulations, the standard for accident and death benefit compensation calculation shall be based on the local average disposable income per annum and resulting in total compensation around USD 150,000, for example.

Then, what can happen if we drive without a valid license? If one of the following acts is committed, the traffic administrative department of the public security organ shall impose a fine of not less than RMB 200 but not more than RMB 2,000:

- driving a motor vehicle without obtaining a motor vehicle driving license, a motor vehicle driving license being revoked, or a motor vehicle driving license being temporarily detained;
- handing over the motorized vehicle to a person who has not obtained a motor vehicle driving license or whose motor vehicle driving license has been revoked or temporarily detained;
- Repeated offenders shall be additionally detained for not more than 15 days.

■ Road Traffic Safety Law of the People's Republic of China (2011 Amendment)
■ Provisions on the Application for and Use of Motor Vehicle Driving Licenses (2016Amendment)

In case of car accident on the road, what should I do?

Anyone encounters car accident in China shall report to the police immediately and inform the insurance company at once. Insurance company will send representative to the spot for investigation and keeping records. The data collected from the related parties shall be passed to the police for recording purpose. Involved parties of the car accident seldom just exchange information only by themselves.

In case of an accident, if it is as minor as a scrape, most people just drive on. If you stop and agree about whatever, you can then continue. For cases involve breakdown of vehicle, the case can be resolved upon the arrival of representatives sent by the insurance company. Please note that if you opt for handling the case by mutual agreement or negotiation between the parties for compensation, your insurance company shall no longer hold responsibility for your case regarding your car accident. Therefore, if you have acquired insurance with enough sum of protection, you shall pass the responsibility to the insurance company and allow them to handle the compensation for you. Please take note that under no circumstances and it is unnecessary shall the parties of car accident leave the scene without first notifying the police and the insurance company. In case of an accident with injury, you must report to police in the first place.

Case Sharing: Hong Kong Container Truck Driver arrested for intentional homicide after hit and run in a fatal accident in China

In Aug 2010, the case of the Hong Kong container truck towing the baby carriage was officially opened for trial at the Shenzhen Intermediate People's Court. Liang Guanxi, the driver and the defendant had no objection to the alleged facts and pleaded guilty in court. The driver claimed fatigue as the cause of the incident and escaped due to terror. A 3-month-old baby, Xiao Menglin was knocked down and the stroller was hoisted into the bottom of the big truck. Alleged driver Liang dragged the baby carriage along with his truck and escaped quickly, leading to a tragic incident. According to the indictment, Liang noticed the baby carriage but did not intend to stop. Rather, Liang escaped quickly and drove at high speed of 80 to 100 kilometers per hour. Liang Guanxi also drove in a S-shaped way, swinging left and right, aiming to get rid of the baby stroller and baby at the bottom. Liang was charged of intentional homicide. Shenzhen Intermediate People's Court made a first-instance judgment on Liang's intentional homicide. He was sentenced to death, suspended for two years and deprived of political rights for life. Such tragic verdict may be avoided if Liang did not escape. As for the offence of regular traffic accident which caused one deceased, the judge would usually adopt 3 years or below fixed-term imprisonment or criminal detention as the starting point. For the sentencing standards for Traffic Accident Crime, if Liang has to be fully responsible, causing death of one person, the starting point of punishment for Liang will generally be fixed-term imprisonment of 3 years and below. In addition, according to the suspended committal order system in China, should the suspended committal order requirements and conditions be met, suspended committal order will be applicable for any fixed-term imprisonment under 3 years (bound over without imprisonment).

The compensation for personal injury of foreigners and stateless persons shall be calculated according to the relevant standards of urban residents. The death compensation is based on the per capita disposable income of urban residents in the previous year of the court where the court is located or the per capita net income of rural residents.

If a traffic accident causes serious injury to more than one person, and all or the main responsibility for the accident, and one of the following circumstances, it shall be convicted and punishable:

- driving the motor vehicle after drinking and taking drugs
- driving without a driving qualification to drive a motor vehicle;
- driving a motor vehicle that is known to be incomplete or has a safety mechanism failure;
- driving without knowing that it is an unlicensed vehicle or a

- motor vehicle that has been scrapped;
- severely overloaded driving;
- to evade the law and pursue the escape from the scene of the accident.

Violation of traffic management regulations, resulting in a major accident, causing serious injury, death or serious losses to public and private property, imprisonment of up to three years or criminal detention shall be imposed.

If the traffic accident has one of the following circumstances, it shall be sentenced to fixed-term imprisonment of not more than three years or criminal detention:

- 1 person who died or 3 persons or more seriously injured, all or mainly responsible for the accident;
- death More than 3 persons shall be responsible for the same accident;
- causing direct loss of public property or property of others, and having full or primary responsibility for the accident, and the inability to compensate for the amount of more than RMB 300,000.

Those who escape or have other particularly bad circumstances shall be sentenced to fixed-term imprisonment of not less than three years and not more than seven years; those who causing death due to escape shall be sentenced to fixed-term imprisonment of not less than seven years.

- Road Traffic Safety Law of the People's Republic of China (2011 Amendment)
- Interpretation of the Supreme People's Court of Some Issues

concerning the Application of Law for the Trial of Cases on Compensation for Personal Injury, 2003
- Criminal Law of the People's Republic of China(2017 Amendment）

How can I claim for compensation if I purchased defective goods or service in China?

In general, consumers who purchased or used defective goods or services and want to complain can negotiate with the merchant in the very first place. Most of the time we have three options, namely, 'Refund, Remake or Repairs'. If the negotiation fails, consumers can file a complaint to consumer council by calling '12315' which is the specific number for consumer complaints throughout China. We heard from time to time stories about Chinese merchants selling or providing defective goods or services to the public in China.

To combat counterfeiting, defective products and to enhance the quality of products, the Chinese government has imposed harsh law in relation to protection of consumer rights. Anti-counterfeiting strategies include if any merchant involves in provision of fraudulent defective products of service to consumers, consumers can request for 3 times of price as compensation. If merchants selling food which violates the food safety standard, consumers can request for 10 times of selling price of goods as compensation. Consumers can request for refund, change of products or maintenance if they have concern on the quality of the purchased items. Such request does not require to be made within 7 days after the purchase. Yet consumers have to raise the issue once they notify the problem. The respective law has also provided examples to illustrate that the burden of proof for different category of defective goods shall be on the manufacturer but not the consumer in order to further protect the rights of the consumers.

Case Sharing: Supermarket in Ningbo selling food with unclear food label fined 10 times of price as compensation to consumer

In 2014, a supermarket in Ningbo was sued by a hawker, Deng for selling food with improper labeling. Deng claimed the supermarket for compensation, requesting the supermarket to refund plus paying 10 times of the selling price of good.

After investigation by the Authorities for Industry and Commerce, it was found that the food was either not properly labelled or was exaggerating the label as promotion strategies, violating the law and regulations in relation to food safety and anti-competition. The supermarket thus then received 4 Administrative Punishments Imposed by Administrative Authorities for Industry and Commerce.

At court hearing, the supermarket suspected the plaintiff as 'Professional extortioner for looking for fraudulent products' and intended to buy the defective products for making profit. The court held that, according to Provisions of the Supreme People's Court on Several Issues Concerning the Application of Law in the Trial of Food and Drug Disputes, the court did not support defense of the seller upon the purchaser's knowledge of the quality of the food or drugs over the disputes regarding the quality of food and drugs. The court supported Deng as regular consumer and ordered the supermarket to refund the fees for the goods in RMB 1,800 RMB and compensate RMB 15,000 to Deng as compensation.

The operator shall guarantee the quality, performance, use and expiration date of the goods or services provided by the goods in the case of normal use of the goods or the service. Even if the consumer noticed the bad quality or under performance of goods and services before purchasing the goods or accepting the service, it will not affect the application of the law. Operators and manufacturers shall guarantee their services and goods to be good at all times.

For consumer durable goods including automobiles, computers, home appliances (refrigerator, air-conditioner, washing machines) or decoration and renovation services, if the customers identify the defects with after purchased the goods or accepted the services within 6 months and then have dispute with the operator or service provider, the burden of proof shall go to the operator or the service provider.

If the operator indicates the quality of the goods or services by advertisement, product description, physical samples or other means, it shall ensure that the actual quality of the goods or services provided by the operator is consistent with the indicated quality.

If the goods or services provided by the operator do not meet the quality requirements, in accordance with the state regulations, the consumer may return the goods or require the operator to fulfill the obligation of replacement, repair, etc.

If the operator provides fraudulent acts on goods or services, it shall increase the compensation for the losses suffered by the consumers according to the requirements of the consumers. The amount of compensation shall be three times the price of the goods purchased by the consumers or the services received. If the total compensation amount is less than RMB 500, the amount will still be RMB 500. Where the law provides otherwise, it shall be in accordance with its provisions.

Anyone who violates the provisions of this Law and has one of the following circumstances shall be divided by the relevant competent department according to their respective duties, and the illegal income, the illegal production and operation of food and the tools, equipment and raw materials used for illegal production and operation shall be confiscated; If the value of the illegally produced and operated food is less than RMB 10,000 the fine will be not less than RMB 2,000 but not more than RMB 50,000; if the value of the goods is more than RMB 10,000, the fine will be at least five times or not less than ten times of the product value. For serious offences, relevant licenses will be confiscated.

- Producing foods from non-food raw materials or adding chemicals other than food additives and other substances that may endanger human health to foods, or using recycled foods as raw materials to produce foods;
- Foods that produce and operate pathogenic microorganisms, pesticide residues, veterinary drug residues, heavy metals, pollutants, and other substances that endanger human health beyond the food safety standards;
- The main and auxiliary foods for infants and young children and other specific groups whose production and management nutrients do not meet the food safety standards;
- Foods that are corrupted by corruption, rancidity of oil, mildew, filth, uncleanness, foreign matter, adulteration, or sensory traits;
- operating poultry, livestock, beasts, aquatic animal meats that

are ill, poisonous or have unknown causes of death, or products that produce diseases such as poultry, livestock, beasts, and aquatic animals that are dying, poisoned or of unknown cause;
- Operating meat that has not been quarantined or quarantined by the animal health supervision agency, or meat products that have not been inspected or tested for unqualified production;
- operating foods that exceed the shelf life;
- Foods that are prohibited from being produced or operated by the state of production and operation for special needs such as disease prevention;
- Using new food materials for food production or to produce new varieties of food additives and food-related products, without safety assessment;
- The food production and operation operator refuse to recall or stop the operation after the relevant competent department orders it to recall or stop the operation of food that does not meet the food safety standards.

Whoever violates the provisions of this Law and causes personal, property or other damage shall be liable for compensation according to law. In case manufacturer producing food that does not meet food safety standards or selling foods that are known to be inconsistent with food safety standards, consumers can request for compensation and are eligible to request the manufacturer or sellers to pay ten times of the price of goods as compensation.

- Law of the People's Republic of China on the Protection of Consumer Rights and Interests (2013 Amendment)
- Product Quality Law of the People's Republic of China (2018 Amendment)

- Food Safety Law of the People's Republic of China (2018 Amendment)

I am not a local Chinese. What do I need to pay attention to when I seek medical advice from hospital in China?

One of the important questions an expatriate in China may want to know is: where to go when getting sick? Major cities like Beijing, Shanghai, Shenzhen have set up a number of high quality international standard hospitals and medical centres which can adequately meet the health needs of the expatriate community. In addition, there are actually many healthcare professionals in China who are graduated from overseas, so it is possible to find English-speaking doctors in China. However, patients in China are required to pay deposit and medical fee prior receiving medical treatment. In most cases, the standard, the hygiene and the environment differ in hospitals of different regions. If any expatriates plan to live in China for good, they shall acquire either local social security insurance, especially medical insurance and insurance for industrial accidents, or any medical insurance applicable for use in China before they enter the country. Foreigners employed in China can participate in social insurance and enjoy social security in accordance with the law.

And, expatriates are suggested to bring a translator or find a doctor who speaks English.

In case of medical negligence, the patient and family members of the patient can negotiate with the hospital. Alternatively, they can also propose to resolve the medical dispute by mediation through administrative measures imposed by the Health Administrative Authority. Of course, they can opt for litigation to protect their own interests.

- Interim Measures for the Participation in Social Insurance of Foreigners Employed in China, 2011
- Measures of Shanghai Municipality on Medical Dispute Prevention and Mediation, 2014

As expatriate, am I eligible to get married in China?

Should any expatriates want to marry Chinese residents, the expatriate shall provide notarized documents to prove his or her marital status as single (with a Single Status Certificate, Affidavit of Single Status, Certificate of No Record of Marriage, Single Status Statutory Declaration, etc.). Applicants can register for marriage at the domicile of either parties with required documents or identification. Once the application is completed, the Marriage Registry (or actually the Civil Affair Bureau) will issue a formal certificate to the applicants.

In China, there are other rules applicants shall take note of such as the legitimate age for marriage. In order to get married, the man shall not be younger than 22 years old and the woman shall not be younger than 20. In case the applicant has not reach the designated age for marriage, the registry for Marriage will reject the application. In China, marriage between same gender is not allowed and is not applicable to law.

Many people may misunderstand foreign-related marriage, believing that the marriage shall be registered in two countries of the domiciles of both the man and the woman to be effective and complete. Indeed, marriage shall be registered once and for all, the same apply to divorce.

The marriage conditions shall apply the law of the domicile of the parties, if the parties have no common domicile, the law of the country of common nationality applies, if the parties have no common nationality, the law of either party's domicile or country of nationality applies.

For the marriage in China's mainland between a Chinese citizen and a foreigner, or between a mainland citizen and a citizen of Hong Kong, Macao, Taiwan, or an overseas Chinese, the man and the woman shall appear together to go through the marriage registration at the marriage registration organization in the habitual residence location of the Mainland citizen.

According to china law, if any of the following circumstances occurs, the marriage shall be invalid:

- if either party is a bigamist;
- if both parties are in the kinship that is forbidden from getting married by law;
- if any party has suffered from any disease that is held by medical science as rending a person unfit for getting married and the disease has not been cured after marriage;
- if any party has not come up to the legitimate age for marriage.

Citizen applying for the marriage registration shall present the following certificates or certification:

- the applicant's residence registration and identification card;
- the signed statement to indicate the applicant has no spouse and the man and the woman are not lineal relatives by blood or collateral relatives by blood up to the third degree of kinship.

Foreigner who applies for marriage registration shall present the following certificates or certification:

- the applicant's valid travel permit, passport and identification card
- the statement notarized by the notary office in the applicant's place of residence that he or she has no spouse and the man, and the woman are not lineal relatives by blood or collateral relatives by blood up to the third degree of kinship.

One further note, if you and your partner are both expatriates, then you can only marry in China if at least one of you is a permanent resident in China.

- Law of the People's Republic of China on Choice of Law for Foreign-related Civil Relationships, 2010
- Marriage Law of the People's Republic of China (2001 Amendment)

I intend to apply divorce with my spouse who is a Chinese, how should I proceed with the application?

In China, there are two types of divorce, either 'consent to the divorce' or 'the divorce is contested'. If any expatriates want to apply divorce in China, one shall consider whether the marriage is registered in China or whether one of the parties is Chinese citizen. There is no prohibition for divorce in China in relation to the length of time of the marriage as in some other countries. For instance, divorce application at English court requires the marriage must last for at least 1 year to satisfy the requirement for applying divorce.

If it is a consent to divorce, meaning the two parties mutually agree to apply divorce, both man and woman can go anytime to the Marriage Registry at the habitual residence of either party to file a joint application.

The parties must bring along an application for divorce and state their reason for divorce to demonstrate there is an irretrievable breakdown of marriage, common reasons include:

- One party to the marriage has committed adultery, or is cohabiting with a third party;
- Domestic violence, or maltreatment and desertion of one party to the marriage by another;
- Bad habits of one spouse for example gambling or drug addiction, which remain persistent despite repeated warnings;
- Separation of the parties for two full years caused by incompatibility;
- Any other circumstances causing alienation of mutual affection between the parties.

The content of the agreement must also include the same views on financial arrangements for children and the distribution of assets and debts. After the registration is completed at the Marriage Registry, a Divorce Certificate (similar to decree nisi in common law court) will be granted to the applicants. This is after, all ancillary matters such as child custody, maintenance and division of matrimonial assets have been determined.

If the parties cannot reach agreement in relation to their divorce, such as disagreement on the distribution of assets, custody of children, ancillary relief, either party shall apply for divorce at the court (the petitioner) in order to protect their personal interests.

In general, foreign-related divorce can be applied in China where one of the parties is domiciled. It is not necessary to apply twice in two countries.

Regarding the marital asset, if there is a valid pre-nuptial agreement in relation to ownership of asset or martial asset agreement, it will be effective in China. The law allows the husband and wife made written agreement in order to share personal asset between the two or distribution of marital asset. Husband and wife may agree that the property acquired during the existence of the marriage relationship and the property before marriage shall be owned by each other, jointly owned or partially owned and partially owned by the parties. The agreement shall be in written form. If there is no agreement or the agreement is not clear, the provisions of Marriage Law shall apply.

Case Sharing: The pre-marital property transfer agreement can be revoked

Mr. Feng and Ms. Wang get married in February 2002. In July of the same year, the two signed a property transfer agreement. Mr. Feng declared that he had transferred a real estate property purchased before his marriage to his wife.

Since the declaration was signed, it was made effective that the real estate property was belonged to Ms. Wang as personal property. Such real estate property was not related to the marital relationship of Feng and Wang and it is not a marital asset. Ms. Wang signed the declaration as 'receiver' of the gift on the declaration. However, according to the property transaction authority, the real estate property was still under Mr. Feng's name. According to Wang, the ownership of the real estate property shall belong to her based on the signed declaration. According to Feng, Wang verbally agreed to pay him RMB 1 Million as the condition to alter the registration at real estate property authority upon signing of the declaration.

The People's Court held that the real estate property was Feng's personal property acquired before marriage. Although Feng agreed to give the real estate property to Wang as gift by agreement, according to law, as a gift relation, , Feng can call off the agreement any time before the title has actually been transferred to the new owner. Apart from public interest including remedies and charity purpose, or agreement to gift in relation to ethnical nature or any notarized agreement of gift, the giver can cancel the gift before the title is transferred. Since the real property of Feng is still under his name, the Court ruled that it is not transferred to new owner that Feng's cancellation of the declaration is legal.

- Law of the People's Republic of China on Choice of Law for Foreign-related Civil Relationships, 2010
- Marriage Law of the People's Republic of China (2001 Amendment)

Is a divorced wife liable for the debts of her ex-husband?

In general, yes. Husband and wife shall be jointly responsible for all the debts during marriage even after they are divorced. According to law, when divorcing, the debts originally borne by the husband and wife shall be jointly repaid. If the joint property is insufficiently paid, or the property belongs to each other, the parties shall arrange a repayment agreement.

Case Sharing: The Court of First Instance ruled Mr. Fang and Ms. Li to pay jointly for 3 million debt

The matter originated from a year ago, due to the gambling habit of a husband, Mr. Fang who has almost lost all the properties, wealth and assets of his family of origin, Ms. Li and Mr. Fang agreed to divorce. The two parties stated in the divorce agreement that the two children and all the rest of the family's property belonged to the woman. The woman shall then be responsible for supporting the family after divorce and the man leaves the family without a penny.

Shortly after the divorce, the court sent a summons to inform Ms. Li that her ex-husband had owed a debt of RMB 3 million in addition to the tens of millions of RMB that had already been lost. Over two years, Ms. Li has discovered the gambling habit of her husband repeatedly. Summons had been sent one after another over the period of the time. Yet, Ms. Li was furious about the new summon as she thought they were divorced, and she should not be responsible to pay for her ex-husband anymore.

However, from the perspective of the creditor, it was an inevitable step to ask Ms. Li to pay the debt as the debt was borrowed to the couple when they were married. The divorce only happened half a month after the money was lend. It was suspicious to the creditor that why the husband and wife were divorced and leaving the husband with no asset? To the creditor, it seemed to be a divorce intended to escape from the debt. If divorce is a solution to escape from debt, then all the creditors must face the risks of total loss in nearly all cases.

Mr. Fang did not appear in the court of first instance and did not submit any evidence. During the court hearing, Ms. Li clearly stated that such huge debt shall not be paid by her. She further claimed that she did not know any details about the debt and did not actually see the money. She insisted that the money had not been used for the family. In the court, Ms. Li said that she was solely responsible for paying all the family expenses before divorce and believed that Mr. Fang did not have to borrow money. Ms. Li stated that when Mr. Fang borrowed the money, he had shared with his friends about the purpose of lending. He said, 'the money was for the operation of his business.' Yet, the money was actually used on internet gambling.

To support her statement, Ms. Li submitted to the court a screenshot of an online gambling website captured on a date before divorce. The screenshot had clearly shown the records of wins and lose of Mr. Fang. However, such records were irrelevant to the RMB 3 million loan.

Ms. Li had also presented a 'guarantee' signed by Mr. Fang on March 2014. In the guarantee, Mr. Fang vowed to quit gambling.

However, it was found that Mr. Fang had immediately borrow RMB 3 million from a friend and most of the money were used for gambling.

In order to prove that the money was gambled and lost by gambling, Ms. Li and her lawyer found it difficult to collect evidence neither from bank nor the police.

Based on the guarantee and other relevant evidence, the court held that 'the divorce was irrelevant to the escape of paying debt.' However, the judge believed that when Mr. Fang borrowed the money from a friend, Mr. Fang and Ms. Li was not divorced. Even though the money was being gambled, the lender did not know such purpose of gambling when lending the money. The lender could therefore assume the money was borrowed to Mr. Fang and Ms. Li jointly as debt during their marriage. Therefore, the court held that whether or not the money was gambled could not be a legitimate defense against the legitimate right of the lender in goodwill.

The court of first instance ruled that the relation of debtor and creditor was valid and ordered Mr. Fang and Ms. Li to pay jointly the debt of RMB 3 million.

Case Sharing: Higher court ruled that Ms. Li is not responsible for the gambling debt of Mr.Fang

Ms. Li refused to accept the judgment of the court of first instance and appealed her case to the Intermediate People's Court in Beijing. During the court hearing, Mr. Fang appeared at the court. During the interrogation of the judge, Mr. Fang admitted that he had used the RMB 3 million on internet gambling. He confessed, ' I started gambling when I visited Macau and lost a few millions of dollars? But Mr. Fang sounded like telling the story of others and he acted calmly when he repeated his tragic story. He further admitted that he has lost money when he gambled on internet, losing the sum of hundreds of the thousands of dollars.

At this stage, Ms. Li who was also presented in the court hearing was relieved. According Article 41 of the Marriage Law of People's Republic of China, either husband of wife who owns debt due to gambling, the debt will not be considered as marital debt as the money was not used for running the family. The debt shall only be paid by either party solely.

The creditor disagreed to the statement of the court. The creditor was a good friend of Mr. Fang and they were estranged since the dispute. The lawyer of the creditor stated that, 'As a good friend Mr. Fang, the creditor helped Mr. Fang when he was in need of money. Yet the creditor was disappointed that Mr. Fang failed to pay the debt' and 'escape to pay by applying divorce.' The creditor regarded Mr. Fang unethical. The creditor insisted that if Mr. Fang has no money, the debt shall be settled by his wife. The judge of the court confirmed the validity of the debt and ordered the debtor to pay the creditor. Yet there was one point to further consider: Does Ms. Li hold the liability to pay?

According to the relevant regulations of the High Court of People, similar cases focused on balancing the interests of both the creditor and the interest of women and children. 'If the spouse of the debtor can show evidence to prove that the loan is irrelevant to the daily expenses of the family and the debtor has bad habit of gambling or drug abuse, then the burden of proof shall go to the debtor alone. If the spouse of the debtor can prove that the money was not used for family expense, the spouse is not responsible to pay the debt. In this case, as Mr. Fang admitted to the court in person that he had gambled the money and Ms. Li presented to the court the screenshot of Mr. Li's gambling record on internet, the court held that the RMB 3 million loan was not used for family expenses to support daily necessities of the family.

Finally, the court in Beijing made the final judgment to overrule the judgment of the Court of First Instance. The court ruled that Mr. Fang had to pay all the loan plus interest within 10 days after the judgment. If Mr. Fang failed to pay, interest would be incurred. Ms. Li should hold no responsibility for the debt of Mr. Fang.

A recent Supreme People's Court document said that only in cases where a loan was taken out under the name of one individual to cover costs beyond the family's daily expenses, then courts shall not hold their spouse, or former spouse, responsible for repaying the money. Therefore, the author suggested that if you want to borrow money during your marriage without affecting your spouse, you shall state clearly that the loan is a personal loan. On the other hand, if you want to lend money to others (couple), please make sure you know the purpose of the money lending and urge both spouses to sign the relevant documents before a loan is granted.

■   Marriage Law of the People's Republic of China (2001 Amendment)

I intend to purchase real estate property in China. The real estate agents introduced 'small-property-rights housing' to me and says they are cheaper. Can I buy them?

The authors advise foreigners in China shall not purchase 'small-property-rights housing' or other non-commercial real estate property not on sale. There is no official definition to 'small-property-rights housing', it generally refers to houses built on rural collective land without paying the land transfer fees. The title ownership certificates are not issued by the Land Department of Government Authority. Instead, the certificate was issued by rural government authority or village government authority. It is an illegal but widespread type of residential development built by villagers on their collectively owned land in suburban areas and urban villages, rural settlements surrounded by modern development in many Chinese cities. The effect of sale and purchase contract of 'small-property-rights housing' is generally considered invalid in the legal practice in China. 'Small-property-rights housing' usually cannot obtain formal housing licenses, thus the future transfer of titles will be uncertain.

In addition, there is no clear regulation on the construction and development of 'small-property-rights housing', which makes it difficult to guarantee the quality of the houses and the after-sales warranty. According to the law, properties cannot be legally transfer include properties with unclear property rights, properties constructed on rural collective land, properties with township property rights, properties with mortgages, properties included in the scope of demolition and construction as well as properties seized by the court under injunction for investigation.

In 2009, the judicial authority in Shenzhen issued a notice forbidding all lawyers to be witness upon signing sale and purchase agreement of 'small-property-rights housing'. Therefore, foreign nationals who wish to purchase 'small-property-rights housing' shall think twice about the legal position and protection.

Case Sharing: Wang and Liu's loan mortgage is valid

On August 20, 2004, Wang borrowed RMB 45,000 from Liu. The two parties signed a loan agreement and registered, and Wang agreed to pay Liu the principal and interest on April 20, 2005. Wang took his two-storey buildings as collateral for the loan. When the loan is due, Liu repeated urged Wang to pay the loan, but Wang always excused himself. On July 21, 2005, Wang sold the house to Zhang for RMB 42,000 and registered the transfer of title and property rights. After Liu knew the situation, he immediately sued Wang in the court and demanded that the purchase and sale between Wang and Zhang to be invalid and his loan agreement with Wang to be valid.

Finally, the court ruled that the sale and purchase of the house between Wang and Zhang was invalid and forced Wang to pay Liu for Liu and Wang had signed a valid registered loan agreement.

- Property Law of the People's Republic of China, 2007
- Land Administration Law of the People's Republic of China (2004 Amendment)

- Interim Regulation of the People's Republic of China on Deed Tax (2019 Amendment)

I owned a real estate property in China and intended to rent it out, what are the risks I should be aware of?

To rent out your real estate property in China, the landlord must request the tenant to provide valid identity card and retain a copy. Landlord and tenant must sign a valid tenant agreement and pay tax to relevant authority for registration.

In addition to leasing terms, deposit and rental fee, the provisions and other aspects worth the attention of both landlord and tenant. The aspects include:

- If the leasing term is over 6 months, formal Tenancy Agreement in written format shall be signed. Leasing without formal agreement will be considered as irregular term of leasing. Both landlord and tenant can terminate the Tenancy Agreement with the irregular-term of leasing anytime at their wishes. Please note that the maximum leasing term is 20 years. Any leasing term over 20 years is invalid.
- The liability for payment of water, electricity, gas and property management fee shall be clearly stated in the Tenancy Agreement.
- The liability of maintenance to the real estate property shall be clearly stated in the Tenancy Agreement. In order to avoid the

disputes between the landlord and the tenant over the breakdown of household items, the Tenancy Agreement shall include the agreed handling methods for malfunction of facilities in the premise either due to natural depreciation on improper usage. In general, there are two circumstances in handling the harm imposed by the tenant against the real estate property. If the tenant had imposed harm to the real estate property under normal use as agreed in the Tenancy Agreement, the tenant shall not be liable to compensation.

- If the tenant did not use the rented property according to agreement or the nature of the property causing loss to the property, the landlord can terminate the tenancy agreement and claim for compensation.
- The termination clause of the tenancy agreement must be specific, including scenarios when the tenant fails to pay rent as agreed, how the landlord can terminate the Tenancy Agreement, or when the tenant has changed the nature of use of the premise, how can the landlord immediate terminate the contract.
- Specify the responsibility for breaching the Tenancy Agreement. This includes the disputable details such as liability of the landlord for not handing over the rented premise to the tenant as agreed in a timely manner, the compensation of landlord to tenant regarding early termination of Tenancy Agreement and the compensation of tenant to landlord regarding early termination of Tenancy Agreement.

According to law, there are scenarios that a tenancy agreement is invalid, for examples:

- If the lessor does not obtain the construction project planning permit or the house that was not constructed in accordance with the construction project planning permit, the lease

contract entered into with the lessee is invalid.
- If the lessor has a temporary construction that has not been approved or has not been constructed in accordance with the approved content, the lease contract concluded with the lessee is invalid.
- The lease term exceeds the service life of the temporary building, and the excess is invalid.

Case Sharing: Tenancy agreement expired. Tenant requested for renewal was rejected

Mr. Li rented out his apartment. When the tenancy agreement was expired, Mr. Li requested to rent the apartment to another new tenant. The tenant refused and requested for renewal of the tenancy agreement without agreeing to the new rental amount suggested by Mr. Li. Indeed, tenants could enjoy the priority to continue the tenancy agreement and the landlord Mr. Li reserved the rights to change the tenancy terms in a reasonable manner. For example, if the rent agreed previously was low, Mr. Li could raise the rental fee up to the standard suggested by the government authority regarding the rent of private housing. Alternatively, if there isn't any standard for reference in some of the region, the landlord can alter a reasonable rental fee with reference to the actual rental rate of the same region in a fair manner. If the existing tenant disagrees to the new rental fee, the tenant shall give up priority to rent the same premise. Mr. Li as landlord, could sign a new tenancy agreement with another new tenant.

- General Provisions of the Civil Law of the People's Republic of China,

2017
- Contract Law of the People's Republic of China, 1999
- Procedures of Shanghai Municipality on the Administration of Residential Tenancy, 2011
- Decision of the People's Government of Shanghai Municipality on Amending the Measures of Shanghai Municipality for the Administration of Residential Tenancy, 2014

The price of real estate property in China goes up and down like roller-coaster ride, what should the buyer do if the seller refuses to complete the transfer procedure when the price goes up?

In recent years, everyone concerns about the news that housing prices in the first-tier cities have skyrocketed. These prices fluctuate a lot and are related to changes in policies, which cause many sellers or buyers to default. When the property price is skyrocketing, the owner sometimes regrets to sell shortly after signing the temporary sale and purchase agreement. What should the buyer do?

It was March 30, 2015 (the Mainland is generally referred to as the '3·30' New Deal), and many local ministries and commissions issued two articles to adjust the relevant policies of the property market. The down payment ratio of the second suite was reduced from 60% to 40%, and the second-hand housing transaction was exempt from business tax. The number of years to keep a property qualifying for transaction tax reduction has been reduced from five years to two years. In short, the new rule is imposed to reduce the difficulty of buying a house and release the purchasing power. When the news came out, the world was full of joy, and the market transactions quickly responded to the policy. This was followed by a continuous surge in house prices in Shenzhen. Many owners in the transaction considered that the cost of default was far lower than the increase in house prices during the period (Note: Generally, the real estate transaction in the mainland takes about 2 to 3 months from the signing of the contract), so there were many default.

Case 1: Judgment of 1st hearing – Dispute over buy and sold of a Shenzhen property

The owner of a Shenzhen apartment Mr. Lee signed an agreement with buyer Mr. Cheung on March 23, 2015 and the owner agreed to sell a 74-square-meter apartment for RMB 2.62 million. After the signing of the agreement, the buyer paid a deposit of RMB 300,000, and the remaining initial payment of RMB 490,000 was jointly funded by the buyer and a bank (loan). The bank also issued a loan commitment letter and promised to issue a loan of RMB 1.83 million.

However, after 2-month time, the buyer did not complete the transaction, the owner Mr. Lee then appointed a lawyer to send a letter to urge the buyer to complete the transaction within seven days. (Please take note that in local second-hand property market, the time required for approval of mortgage and the transaction duration depend very much on the bank, not the individual.) The buyer failed to complete the transaction according to schedule.

The owner then proposed to terminate the contract on the grounds that the transaction was not completed on time, and by the end of June, the owner then sold the properties to another buyer Mr. Wang at higher price.

At the time of the 1st selling the house with Mr. Cheung, the unit price of the house involved was about RMB 35,000 per square meter. In the new deal with Mr. Wang, the unit price of the real estate had jumped to between RMB 40,000 and RMB 50,000 per square meter. Taking this 74 square meter property as an example, the total price had climbed over RMB 1 million.

Due to the price fluctuation in property market, sometimes landlords in China choose to find a reason to terminate a contract when the price of property climbs like rocket. In any case (include cases in which the reason is illegitimate) if the seller fails to complete the transaction; the buyer can ask the seller to pay liquidated damages. The liquidated damages are normally amount to the deposit or 20% of the total contract sum. In this case, the properties involved in the transaction worth RMB 2.26 million. If the owner Mr. Lee breaks the contract, he has to pay a compensation to the amount of deposit or 20% of the lump sum to Mr. Cheung, which is RMB 524,000. But since the property price had climbed up for RMB 1 million in a short period of time, even the owner Mr. Lee may lose in the litigation case with Mr. Cheung, he can still earn hundreds of thousands after compensation paid in breach of first contract.

Case 2: Judgment of 2nd hearing - Dispute over buy and sold of a Shenzhen property

The above case wasnot a single incident in China, and there was an increasing number of buyers or sellers speculating in the properties market and breaching the contract intentionally. The court's judgment had also changed due to the increasing number of seller defaults caused by rising house prices. Since 2015, in the second hearing of the case between Mr. Lee and Mr. Cheung regarding their dispute on the transaction of a Shenzhen apartment, Court began to rule that either the parties need to continue and complete the transaction, or the seller to pay an increased amount of the liquidated damages to the buyer. In other words, the parties may face additional cost of breaching the contracts. The judge's move was to increase the cost of default significantly. So, parties shall understand their own liability before entering a contract, consult a lawyer and study the latest relevant cases and judgments of the court before they intend to breach a contract.

- General Provisions of the Civil Law of the People's Republic of China, 2017
- Contract Law of the People's Republic of China, 1999
- The Civil Procedure Law of the People's Republic of China (2017 Revision)

My dad has just passed away. How should I proceed the application if I want to succeed his deposits in China bank accounts and two apartments?

With the increasing number of expatriates coming to China over the years to invest, work and live, issues concerning succession are becoming more common, especially for those who have developed a business or have purchased property in the country.

Succession in China relies on will if there was a valid will. A will is considered formed if the testamentary form conforms to the law of the habitual residence of the testator when one creates the will or when one dies, or to the law of his nationality, or to the law of the place where the act of creating the will occurs. The effect of a will is governed by the habitual residence of the deceased when one creates the will or when one dies, or by the law of one's nationality. Matters of estate administration, etc. are governed by the law of the place where the estate locates. Noted Rights in rem in immovable property is governed by the law of the place where the immovable property locates.

If the deceased die as an intestate ('intestate' includes a person who leaves without a will, or also known as statutory succession), residuary estate of the deceased will be distributed to all the beneficiaries according to law. For succession to estate on intestacy, please note that the distribution in succession in China is unique and may differ from that of many other countries. In China, the residuary estate of an intestate shall be distributed in the following order:

- First in order: surviving husband or wife, children, parents.
- Second in order: brothers and sisters, paternal grandparents, maternal grandparents.

The successor(s) first in order shall inherit to the exclusion of the successor(s) second in order. The successor(s) second in order shall inherit in default of any successor first in order. The 'children' referred to in this Law include legitimate children, illegitimate children and adopted children, as well as stepchildren who supported or were supported by the decedent. The 'parents' referred to in this law include natural parents and adoptive parents, as well as stepparents who supported or were supported by the decedent. The 'brothers and sisters' referred to in this Law include blood brothers and sisters, brothers and sisters of half-blood, adopted brothers and sisters, as well as stepbrothers and stepsisters who supported or were supported by the decedent. The share distributed among the legitimate successors shall be equal.

Statutory succession is governed by the law of the habitual residence of the deceased when he or she dies. However, statutory succession of immovable property is governed by the law where the immovable property locates.

To succeed a real estate property (housing) in China, required documents include identification documents of the legitimate successors. If some of the legitimate successors are deceased, death certificate shall be provided. Legitimate successors shall prepare all the required documents and present to notary office assisted by lawyers. For those who wish to give up their succession rights shall also be presented in the notary office. All the legitimate successors are required to be presented at the notary office. If any of the successors or deceased are foreigners, they shall go to the notary office of their own country for legalization and authentication before presenting himself / herself at the notary office in China to notarize the proof of relationship and present the notarized documents to the notary office located at where the real estate property is located. After all the notarization procedures are completed, the deceased can apply for transfer of the real estate property under the name of new owner.

To succeed bank deposits in Mainland Bank Account, the legitimate successor shall prepare all the relevant documents and present them to the notary office where the bank is located and operated or are sometimes required to present the documents to the People's Court and apply for Certificate of Inheritance. By presenting the Certificate of Inheritance approved by the court, the successor can request the bank to transfer the deposits of the deceased to the legal successor(s).

Expatriates holding assets in China are advised to make provisions in accordance with Chinese succession law through a Chinese or Bilingual will to define the distribution of assets located in China in case of any misfortune.

- Law of Succession of the People's Republic of China, 1985
- Answers of the Higher People Court of Beijing to Certain Difficult Problems concerning Trial of Cases Involving Succession Disputes, 2018
- Law of the People's Republic of China on Choice of Law for Foreign-related Civil Relationships, 2010

My assets in China shall only belong to my sons and daughters in the future?

Many foreigners or overseas Chinese would invest in real estate property for self-use or as an investment in China. However, most of the investors may overlook the problems in relation to succession of having real estate property in China. By sharing of the following example, you may understand more about the underlying problem. In short, it is concluded that your sons or daughters may not be the only beneficiaries of your assets when you are deceased and your real estate properties in China may not be distributed only to them.

Case Sharing: Who will succeed the RMB 8 million inheritance?

Xiao Ming is the only son of an American Chinese family. Xiao Ming parents had purchased a 150-square-meter real estate property in Nanshan of Shenzhen worth 8 million registered under the name of Xiao Ming's father. Xiao Ming's father was deceased a few years ago and his mother was deceased recently. Xiao Ming rarely went back to China, but he realized that the price of real estate property in China of his parents is high enough for him to sell and cash out. He intended to apply for transfer of the real estate property under his name.

- Law of People's Republic of China applicable

Any American succeeding real estate property in China is exclusively under the jurisdiction of the People's Court of where the real estate property is located. Thus, the law of People Republic of China applies. Xiao Ming was aware of such law and understood that the succession application should be filed in China. Xiao Ming thus prepared all the relevant required documents and went to relevant government department to apply for transfer of property under his name. Xiao Ming further enquired the Housing Authority for the statutory requirements or Court's judgment to fulfil the requirement of his application.

- Xiao Ming was being rejected for his application

Xiao Ming presented the real estate warranty, death certificates of his parents (2 deceased), certificate of estate executor to the Housing Authority in China to apply for transfer of title (real estate property) under his name as legal successor. However, the Housing Authority in China replied to Xiao Ming that he could not applied the transfer by only presenting those documents, proper legalization is requested. Xiao Ming could only go back the States and assigned other time for the application. After he googled and sought advice from friends, Xiao Ming thought there should not be any disputes in relation to his succession of his parent's real estate property and he did not believe that the case shall be brought to the court. He then arranged another time to visit a notary office in China.

- Request for notarization being rejected

When Xiao Ming went to the notary office to apply for notarization, the staff in the notary office requested him to invite all the relatives of his parents to present in the notary office so that the notary office can issue the certificate. Yet, Xiao Ming realized that his parents have a lot of relatives in both United States and China (some in Hong Kong) who have lost connection with him. He then had the question came in mind: how and where can I find them all to come along with me to this notary office all at once? In addition, the staff reminded Xiao Ming that the requirement for the details of the notarization certificate. Xiao Ming was very disappointed and left the notary office.

At this moment, Xiao Ming may feel that it is annoying and complicated to go through the relevant procedures in China. He even thought that the notary office and relevant organization deliberately hindered him from a smooth application. Yet, after you understand the following analysis and you would probably understand the logic of the staff of the notary office or the Housing Authority. To conclude, according the Succession Law of the People's Republic of China, the real estate property of Xiao Ming's parent does not belong to Xiao Ming only. There are at least 8 more legal successors for the real estate property according to law. You may refer to the following chart for details.

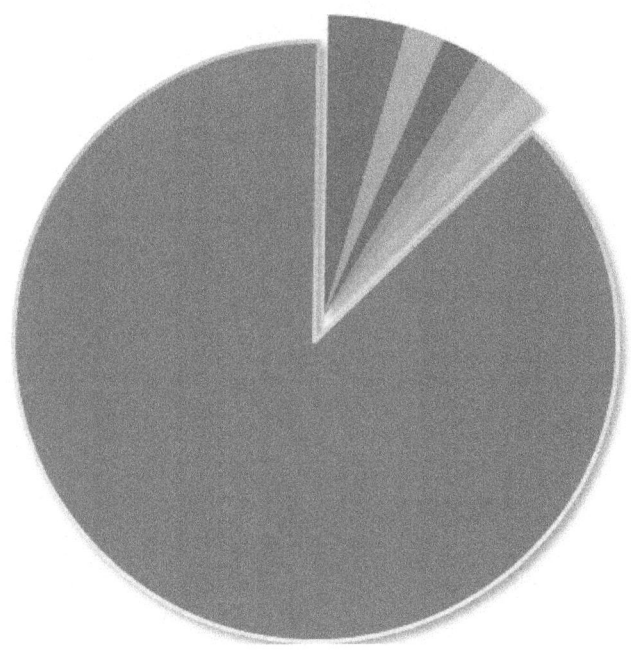

Xiao Ming (7/8)
Sister of dad, Spouse of sister of dad (1/24)
Elder Brother of dad (1/48)
Spouse of Elder Brother of dad (1/48)
Son of Second elder brother of dad, A (1/72)
Son of Second elder brother of dad, B (1/72)
Daughter of Second elder brother of dad, C (1/72)

- Case analysis

Brief description of the Xiao Ming family situation:

- Xiao Ming's parents got married in the United States in 1980, Xiao Ming is the only son.

- The property in China was purchased in 2000 under the name of Xiao Ming's father.

- Xiao Ming's father died in the United States in an accident in 2007.

- Xiao Ming's father has no will followed by the death of his due to illness without will but verbally inform Xiao Ming that the property belongs to him after her death.

- Xiao Ming's father died after his grandfather. Grandmother of Xiao Ming died a few years after his father

- Xiao Ming's father has four siblings and his dad was the third.

- Elder brother of Xiao Ming's father is alive and divorced. Ex-spouse of elder brother of Xiao Ming's father is alive. They have two children in Hong Kong

- Second brother of Xiao Ming's father died before his father, spouse of second brother of Xiao Ming is alive. They have three children, one in China, two in the United States.

- Xiao Ming has no connection with the younger sister of his father and the spouse of his father's younger sister. Xiao Ming does not understand the family situation of this auntie and uncle

- When Xiao Ming's mother died, his grandparents are deceased.

According the Law of People's Republic of China, the real estate property shall not be inherited by Xiao Ming solely unless the other legal successors agreed to give up their succession rights at notary office in China. The actual succession of Xiao Ming should be calculated based on the following facts:

- This house is the common property of Xiao Ming's parents during his marriage. Xiao Ming's father died. Half of this house belongs to Xiao Ming's mother and half belongs to Xiao Ming's father's legacy.
- When Xiao Ming's father died, there were three legal heirs, namely Xiao Ming's mother, Xiao Ming, and Xiao Ming's grandparents. According to Chinese law, the order of succession for the legal successor should goes in this order: person in the first order includes spouse, children and parents. If there are no specific circumstances, the property will be distributed evenly upon the ½. Therefore, Xiao Ming's mother can succeed the first 1/2 plus 1/6, 2/3 in total. Xiao Ming can succeed 1/6 and his grandmother 1/6.
- After Xiao Ming's grandmother died, her 1/6 will be succeeded by 4 siblings of Xiao Ming's father, each 1/24.
- The 1/24 of the elder brother of Xiao Ming's father should be counted as asset within the marriage. After divorce, 1/24 should be split into half, thus elder brother of Xiao Ming's father succeeds 1/48 and ex-spouse 1/48
- The second elder brother of Xiao Ming's father and Xiao Ming's father died before his grandmother, according to law, the property of The second elder brother of Xiao Ming's father and Xiao Ming's father should go to the next generation with direct blood relation, which the 1/24 of The second elder brother of Xiao Ming's father should be distributed evenly to the three children, each with 1/72, the 1/24 should be distributed to Xiao Ming. In addition to the 1/6 mentioned earlier, Xiao Ming shall succeed 5/24 of the real estate property.
- The sister of Xiao Ming's father is not divorced; thus, the couple can succeed 1/24.
- Xiao Ming's mother was deceased; therefore, all her estate shall go to Xiao Ming. Xiao Ming can succeed 5/24 + 2/3 = 7/8.

Such examples in related to succession in China is not uncommon. Therefore, if you are owner of any real estate property in China, you should consider plan it ahead in how to transfer the real estate property or make the succession effective when you are still alive. Again, a will prepared in accordance with Chinese succession laws will be a good idea.

- Law of Succession of the People's Republic of China, 1985
- Law of the People's Republic of China on Choice of Law for Foreign-related Civil Relationships, 2010

What are the ways to transfer my apartment in China under the name of my kids?

There are three main ways to change the owner (title) of a foreign-related property, including sales and purchase, gifts and succession:

1. By Sale and Purchase. To change the name of the owner of a foreign-related property, foreign applicants shall pay the fee for notarization documents for sales and purchase, property tax, personal tax and tax for deed. Some of the tax fees can be waived subject to the policies of the government
2. As gift. To change the name of the owner of a foreign-related property by way of giving, foreign applicants shall pay the fee for notarization documents for sales and purchase, property tax, personal tax and tax for deed and presented the proof for family relationship and pay the fee for notarization of such evidence.

3. By way of succession. Such method involves only fees for notarization, but it required the cooperation of all the legal successors. Among all, handling the real estate of next of kin who is alive will consider two methods which are gifts and transfer of real estate property. Apart from the cost emerged out of the transfer application, you should also consider what the next step to handle the property is. Whether or not the property will be sold after the transfer of title. If you do not intend to sell the property, it may be more cost-effective to transfer the property by way of giving. But if you intend to sell the property after the transfer of title, 20% of the personal tax shall be paid upon the property is sold. In that case, it is more cost-effective to transfer by sales and purchase rather than gifting.

In most cases, buy and sell is a cost-effective way to transfer a title (even between blood line and relatives).

- Law of Succession of the People's Republic of China, 1985
- Notary Law of the People's Republic of China (2017 Amendment)
- Notice of the Ministry of Finance and the State Administration of Taxation on Issues Concerning the Tax Basis for Calculating Deed Tax, Property Tax, Land Value-Added Tax, and Individual Income Tax after Replacing Business Tax with Value-Added Tax, 2016
- Announcement No. 75 [2015] of the State Administration of Taxation—Announcement on Further Simplifying and Regulating the Certification Materials as Required for Exemption of Business Tax and Individual Income Tax on the Real Estates Granted Gratuitously as Gifts or Accepted as Donations by Individuals, 2015

PART IV Frequently Asked Questions on Chinese Law

What happens if I get caught working illegally in China?

Isn't it obvious? You will end up with big penalty, detained, blacklisted and deported if you break China's visa and immigration rules.

You must apply for a work permit before you start working in China. The following are examples of breaking the rules:

- Working full time or PART TIME in China without working permit.
- Applying working permit with ONE company while you are actually working with ANOTHER.
- Working in China AFTER your working permit has expired.
- Your spouse holding Q visa work in China.

You will be ordered to exit the country immediately if you violate the visa type/condition or deported if you work illegally in China. Furthermore, a penalty between RMB 5,000 and RMB 20,000 where the exact amount is at discretion of the police, plus a possible detainment between 5 to 15 days will be imposed.

It all depends on how serious of your violation and whether you are intentional or unintentional (the first decision will be based on the judgment of the police!). The company who recruited illegal workers will be fined between RMB 10,000 (per head) up to RMB 100,000, and any illegal income they have made will be confiscated.

So, what to do if I get caught? First things first, call your lawyer. In most of the cases, you will be better understood and possibly more sympathetic by the authorities via a local lawyer. Please try to be cooperative and polite with the police, explain why you are breaking the law unintentionally. Most of the time, the police will decide what to do with you, which means they can make the case either easier or harder at their discretion.

You will be penalized for illegal working, and furthermore, it will leave you a bad record at customs which thereafter cause major problems with your next visa application. Therefore, please properly apply for a valid permit if you intend to work or stay in China. Nowadays, it is not difficult and, in most cases, only a matter of procedures to apply one. Even self-employment by your own company is acceptable.

When foreigners engage in activities not corresponding to the purposes of stay or residence, or otherwise violate the laws or regulations of China, which makes them no longer eligible to stay or reside in China, they may be ordered to exit China within a time limit. Where a foreigner's violation of this Law is serious but does not constitute a crime, the Ministry of Public Security may deport them. The penalty decision made by the Ministry of Public Security shall be final.

One should note that a deported foreigner shall not be allowed to enter China within 10 years calculating from the date of deportation, according to law.

Case Sharing: Foreigners working illegally in Shanghai

It was the night before Christmas in 2015, there was a cleaning of house and illegal foreign teachers were nestled all snug in their bars. According to the news posted on various expat forums on Christmas Day, at least 50 foreigners were rounded up by Shanghai authorities during a Christmas Eve sting operation to catch expats working illegally in the city, where amateur teachers were attracted by an ad for RMB 20,000(USD 3,035) a week ESL teacher job, and the company (unlicensed school) involved had been illegally hiring foreigners on tourist visas from time to time.

- Provisions on the Employment of Foreigners in China (2010 Amendment)
- Exit and Entry Administration of the People's Republic of China, 2012
- Labor Law of the People's Republic of China (2018 Amendment)

When expatriates breaking law in China, will they be treated differently?

In general, the law governing foreigners in China is based on the principle of jus soli. Jus soli is Latin legal term meaning 'right of the soil'. Therefore, for foreigners who are prosecuted by judicial authorities in China, the criminal law of China applies. Foreigners in China involving civil disputes or criminal offences and resulted in detention, arrest or facilities for enforcement, trials or criminal penalty shall enjoy the same rights, responsibilities and liabilities as residents of China, save and except foreigners who has Diplomatic immunity or other immunity. In addition, foreigners are entitled to consular visits. Vienna Convention on Consular Relations 1963 sets the rules for consular visits for countries based on the international law. On 20 Jun 1995, 'Regulations Concerning Certain Issues in relation to Foreign-related Cases' issued by The Ministry of Foreign Affairs of the People's Republic of China, The Supreme People's Court, The Supreme People's Procuratorate of the People's Republic of China, Ministry of Public Security of the People's Republic of China, Ministry of State Security and Ministry of Justice of the People's Republic of China has set the direction for the consulate visits for all criminal cases different stages of the legal proceedings. Consular visits will be arranged for foreigners at least once a month unless otherwise stated in the terms and conditions of the consulates. At the moment, most of the countries do not have any special arrangements with China in relation to criminal judicial procedures. In extreme cases, if foreigners who commits crime in China and escapes to their own country, they will be arrested and prosecuted by overseas judicial authorities based on the principle of jus sanguinis. Jus sanguinis is the Latin legal term meaning 'right of blood'.

According to civil procedure law and criminal procedure law of China, foreign nationals, foreign enterprises and organizations which institute or respond to actions in the people's courts shall have equal procedural rights and obligations as citizens, legal entities and organizations of the People's Republic of China.

Case Sharing: Drug bust involving foreigners

In 2019, Canadians was arrested in the eastern Chinese city of Yantai, according to Global Affairs Canada, the country's foreign ministry. The Canadian being held in custody had received consular services, and the detention of the Canadian occurred at about the same time as the arrest of a number of foreign teachers and students on drug charges in the city of Xuzhou, also in eastern China. At least four of the 16 arrested in Xuzhou were British teachers, according to the British Embassy in Beijing. According to news, the police in Xuzhou said one of the arrested foreigners had been criminally detained, which means the individual is likely to face formal charges. The rest had been placed under administrative detention, which, under Chinese law, should not last more than 15 days.

It worth to highlight that drug convictions can attract long prison sentences in China, including the death penalty in cases of trafficking.

- The Civil Procedure Law of the People's Republic of China (2017 Revision)
- Criminal Procedure Law of the People's Republic of China (2018 Amendment)

My money in my China bank account has been wrongly transferred to the swindler. What should I do?

Telephone fraudulent case happens from time to time. When you realized your money in the bank had been transferred to swindler, what could you do apart from calling the police and the bank? Rumors in the internet had suggested two self-help remedies for people whose bank account or credit card were stolen in China: 1. Repeatedly input wrong password on your online banking account and make your account frozen so that you can gain time to stop the thief, 2. When your received the payment message from the bank showing your credit card is being stolen and credited elsewhere in another city or outside China, you may cash out money from the card at the same time immediately to prove that 'the credit card is in China yet being stolen and credited outside China'. Let us explain to you the function of such two remedies: the suggestion for entering the wrong password at internet banking in which you noticed that your card is being stolen by swindler refers to your immediate action to login to internet banking or phone banking and enter wrong password deliberately, the relative account will be frozen to avoid the swindler from withdrawing the money. Please note that such remedy may immediately help you in freezing the internet account or phone banking account but not necessary the ATM system or the bank counter service. Therefore, informing the bank and report to the police are inevitable and more effective.

Some may suggest that in order to 'retain the evidence as proof on the spot', if any message from the bank informing the cardholder that the credit card is being used somewhere else not in your present city, the cardholder shall go to the nearest ATM to withdraw RMB 100 or spend at the nearest merchants in China with receipts as evidence to prove that the card is with the cardholder while overseas (other cities) transaction is made before reporting to the police. They believe that such action can help showing evidence to the police or the court and can claim the compensation or sue the swindler at court later and the bank shall be responsible for such loss. Such suggestion is correct to prove that the card being credited is still in your present city (In China, the burden of proof is on the plaintiff, so it is important to obtain evidence). So the author agrees that If any credit card is being stolen for use elsewhere in the world, one of the effective ways to prove that the card is still in China is to use the card immediately at the merchant nearby in order to prove that the transaction is not made by the cardholder. A better way in retaining evidence is to use the credit card immediately to prove that the card is still with you and spend in front of some witnesses. If you are working in the office or at some public places and the credit card is with you, you may immediately go to the bank and call 110 showing your card to the bank staff and the police. This will be a stronger evidence. Most of the bank will advise its customers whose card is being stolen and transaction was made overseas to call the customer service for reporting the loss of card and stop the card from being misused. To further protect yourself from stolen card transaction, it is suggested that cardholder shall always keep the information of the credit card such as the card number, password, expiry date and CVS number. According to the staff of the bank, when you are forced to draw from ATM by gangster, please take note to the CCTV system located in the bank, at the ATM, by the road, etc. Allow the gangster to show his face in front of the CCTV system to safeguard your personal security. Those records will further assist the police to tackle the case.

In 8 Apr 2011, according to the Interpretation of the Supreme People's Court and the Supreme People's Procuratorate on Several Issues Concerning the Specific Application of Law in Handling Criminal Cases of Fraud, the value of personal and public property worth RMB 3,000 to over RMB 10,000 and from RMB 30,000 to over RMB 100,000 and RMB 500,000 will be considered as 'relatively big sum in amount' and 'big sum in amount' and 'enormously big sum in amount', which determine the length of sentence for committing the crime.

According to law, if a large amount of public and private property is defrauded, one shall be sentenced to fixed-term imprisonment of not more than three years, criminal detention or control, and shall be punished with a fine or a single penalty; if the amount is huge or there are other serious circumstances, the penalty shall be between three years and less than ten years, with a fixed-term imprisonment and fines; if the amount is extremely large or there are other particularly serious circumstances, he shall be sentenced to fixed-term imprisonment of not less than ten years or life imprisonment and shall be fined or confiscated.

To prevent falling to this kind of scam. Here are a few tips:

- Remember that just because someone knows some personal details, such as your name, ID and address, doesn't mean they are genuine.
- Banks or trusted organizations such as the police will never contact you asking you to give your PIN or full password, or transfer money to another account.
- Double check your business partner over the phone every time you receive a payment request via email, it could be from hackers.
- Always question uninvited approaches asking for information, they could be scams.
- Never automatically click on a link in an unexpected email or text.

■ Criminal Law of the People's Republic of China(2017 Amendment）

Is it illegal to play mahjong or cards in China?

Gambling is illegal under Chinese law, any form of gambling, including online-gambling, gambling overseas, or opening casinos overseas to attract citizens of China as primary customers, is considered illegal.

Case Sharing: Remarks by Chinese Embassy Spokesperson on Issues of Chinese Citizens concerning Gambling in the Philippines (2019/08/08)

The Chinese Embassy has taken note of recent remarks by Philippine Amusement and Gaming Corp. (PAGOR) vice president Jose Tria that Chinese working in Philippine offshore gaming operators (POGOs) will be transferred to 'self-contained' communities or hubs. The Chinese Embassy expresses its grave concern over such potential move by PAGOR, which may infringe on the basic legal rights of the Chinese citizens concerned, and strongly urges the Philippine government to effectively protect the legitimate rights and interests of Chinese citizens in the Philippines.

In the remarks made by the Chinese Embassy related to the operation of Philippine Amusement and Gaming Corp (PAGOR), it was highlighted that any forms of gambling including online-gambling, overseas gambling operators or anyone operating overseas casinos targeting Chinese citizens as customers is illegal according to the Chinese law and regulations. Casinos, offshore gambling operators, Philippine Offshore Gaming Operators (POGOs) and other gambling entities in the Philippine are target Chinese citizens as their primary customers causing a large number of Chinese citizens being recruited and hired in the Philippine gambling industry.

According to the Chinese laws and regulations, any form of gambling by Chinese citizens, including online-gambling, gambling overseas, opening casinos overseas to attract citizens of China as primary customers, is illegal. The casinos and offshore gaming operators (POGOs) and other forms of gambling entities in the Philippine target Chinese citizens as their primary customers. A large number of Chinese citizens have been illegally recruited and hired in the Philippine gambling industry. In many cases, the employers of Philippine casinos, POGOs and other forms of gambling entities do not apply necessary legal work permits for their Chinese employees. Some Chinese citizens are even lured into and cheated to work illegally with only tourist visas.

The fact that the Philippine casinos and POGOs and other forms of gambling entities are targeting Chinese customers has severely affected the Chinese side in the following aspects:

- Huge amount of Chinese funds has illegally flown out of China and illegally into the Philippines, involving crimes such as cross-border money laundering through underground banking, which undermines China's financial supervision and financial security. A conservative estimate shows that gambling-related funds flowing illegally out China and into the Philippines amounts to hundreds of millions of Chinese Yuan(Renminbi) every year. There are analysts who believe that part of the illegal gambling funds has flown into local real estate markets and and other sectors in the Philippines.
- The fact that a large number of Chinese citizens are lured into illegal gambling has resulted in an increase of crimes and social

problems in China. In particular, some gambling crimes and telecom frauds are closely connected, which has caused huge losses to the victims and their families.
- Many of the Chinese citizens working illegally in Philippine casinos or POGOs and other forms of gambling entities are subjected to what media described as 'modern slavery' due to severe limitation of their personal freedom. Their passports are taken away or confiscated by the Philippine employers. They are confined to live and work in certain designated places and some of them have been subjected to extortion, physical abuse and torture as well as other ill-treatments. At the same time, dozens of kidnappings and tortured cases of Chinese citizens who gamble or work illegally in gambling entities in the Philippines have taken place. Some Chinese citizens were physically tortured, injured or even murdered.

The Chinese Government attaches great importance to the crackdown on cross-border gambling activities. The Ministry of Public Security of China has taken many actions and will carry out more special operations aimed at preventing and combating the cross-border gambling. China will focus on investigating and cracking some major cases, including those of organizing gambling overseas and opening online gaming, and will destroy networks of criminal organizations involved in recruiting gamblers from China by overseas casinos and using the Internet to open casinos in China. China will also crack down on 'underground banks' and online payment platforms that provide a financial settlement for cross-border gambling and other crimes, and wipe out domestic network operators and companies that provide technical support for such crimes.

The Judicial Interpretation of the Relevant Laws on the Application of Online-gambling Crimes jointly issued by China's Supreme

People's Court and the Supreme People's Procuratorate clearly stipulates that Chinese citizens gambling overseas, opening casinos to attract Chinese citizens as primary customers may constitute gambling crimes. Criminal liability can be pursued in accordance with the provisions of the Criminal Law of China.

The Judicial Interpretation of the Relevant Laws on the Application of Online-gambling Crimes jointly issued by China's Supreme People's Court and the Supreme People's Procuratorate clearly stipulates that Chinese citizens gambling overseas, opening casinos to attract Chinese citizens as primary customers may constitute gambling crimes. Criminal liability can be pursued in accordance with the provisions of the Criminal Law of China.

So, is it legal to play mahjong in China? It depends. Playing mahjong is one of the most popular activities during the festivals or holidays. Yet, playing mahjong or cards can be a crime.

According to law, anyone who facilitates gambling for the purpose of making profits or participates in any gambling activity on a relatively large sum of gambling stakes shall be detained for not more than 5 days or shall be fined not more than RMB 500. If the circumstances are serious, one will be detained for not less than 10 days but not more than 15 days and shall be concurrently fined not less than RMB 500 but not more than RMB 3, 000.

Therefore, whether gamblers are breaking the law, it all depends how much they gamble.

So, what is the definition of 'gambling involving big sum of gambling fund'? According to the Law of the People's Republic of China on Public Security Administration, there isn't a standardized definition of 'big sum of gambling fund' but different standards in different regions of China. Below are some examples:

- Beijing: personal gambling fund of over RMB 300 but less than RMB 500 will be fined for not more than RMB 500. Gambling fund of RMB 500 to RMB 1,500, gamblers shall be detained for not more than 5 days.
- Shenzhen: personal gamble fund over RMB 500 is considered to be big sum of gambling fund
- Hebei: According to Public Security Organs Administrative Punishment Standard in Hebei defines big sum of gambling fund to be over RMB 200.
- Shangdong: According to Shandong Public Security Bureau standard, it stipulates that 'gambling involving a big sum of gambling fund' refers to the personal gambling amount of over RMB 100 or over RMB 400 on the spot.
- Jiangsu: Jiangsu Provinces stipulates that the starting point for punishment regarding gambling fund should be over RMB 200 per person. For gambling fund over RMB 200 but less than RMB 1,000, the fine will be under RMB 500. Personal gambling fund or individual gambling fund of over RMB 1,000 but under RMB 3,000, the gamblers shall be detained for not over 5 days.
- Sichuan: The Sichuan Province stipulates according to the Sichuan Province Public Security Department standard, gambling fund on the spot of over RMB 1,000 but less than RMB 4,000 is defined to be big amount of gambling fund.

Case Sharing: Illegal Gambling

The definition of 'gambling fund' will be different according to the real situation. In 2015, there is a case involving mahjong gambling of Mr. Fang. The mahjong game involves gambling fund from RMB 10 to RMB 60 or more per game for losers and RMB 30 to RMB 300 per game for winners. The court held that the mahjong game of Fang and the other 3 was an activity with betting of big sum of amount with small amount of gambling fund. The court also considered that there were over RMB 800 captured on the spot. Considering the two factors, the court held that the situation of Fang was considered to be 'big sum of gambling fund' and the gamblers shall be detained for punishment.

- Criminal Law of the People's Republic of China(2017 Amendment）
- Public Security Administration Punishments Law of the People's Republic of China (2012 Amendment)

What should I do if my pet bites others?

Expatriates love pets. Yet, pets may sometimes cause risks and cause injuries to others. If you are a pet lover, you are assumed to have good control over your pets. In China, there aren't any rules to spoil pets hurting people, yet pet owners will be eligible for responsibility and compensation. According to PRC law, if any pet cause injury to others, the pet owners or the caretaker of the pets shall be liable to tort offence. The caretakers or pet owners may not be liable to any responsibility only when one can prove that the tort offence is caused by intentional acts or gross negligence of the infringed parties.

If a domesticated animal causes harm to any person, its keeper or manager shall bear civil liability. If the harm occurs through the fault of the victim, the keeper or manager shall not bear civil liability; if the harm occurs through the fault of a third party, the third party shall bear civil liability. The keeper may not be liable if it can be proven that the damage was caused by an intentional act or gross negligence on the part of the infringed.

According to law, anyone who interferes with the normal life of any other person due to animal breeding shall be given a warning. If he fails to make corrections after the warning, or if he indulges his animal to frighten any other person, one will be fined not less than RMB 200 but not more than RMB 500. Anyone who provokes an animal to injure any other person shall be punished.

In other words, in most cases the pet owners or caretakers have to be responsible for compensation unless they can prove that the victim has intentionally agitated or provoked the pet. If your pet has run into serious trouble, please seek help from professionals for legal advice.

Case Sharing: Dog owner pay USD6,660 compensation to Lamborghini driver who hit her golden retriever

According to the news 2018, a dog owner has agreed to pay a Lamborghini owner RMB 45,000(USD6,600) as compensation after her dog ran out in front of the car and caused minor damage to the vehicle.

The golden retriever escaped with minor injuries when it ran into the road and was hit by the sports car in Suzhou, Jiangsu Television reported. The animal ran off after it slipped its leash while it was being walked by the owner's 13-year-old daughter. The golden retriever was only slightly injured but the RMB 8 million car was left with a damaged side vent, which costs an estimated RMB 450,000 to repair.

The report said that the driver had initially offered the girl RMB 2,000 to pay for the dog's veterinary bills, but the girl called her mother, who then insisted on calling police.

Under Chinese law, the pet owner Ms. Zhou could have been liable for the full cost of the repairs because she had failed to keep the animal under control. However, officers mediated an agreement between the dog owner and the driver, Mr. Wang, who agreed to accept a tenth of the total.

Mr. Wang wrote on Weibo: 'It's impracticable and may hurt the family if I ask them to pay all the costs, so I chose mediation with the dog owner. And the dog owner said she also wanted her daughter to learn a lesson thus she paid me RMB 45,000as compensation.'

- Tort Law of the People's Republic of China, 2009
- Public Security Administration Punishments Law of the People's Republic of China (2012 Amendment)
- General Provisions of the Civil Law of the People's Republic of China, 2017

I heard that private lending in China is illegal, isn't it?

Generally speaking, private lending in China is not illegal. In practice, the People's Court will apply the relevant provisions of the

Civil Law of the People's Republic of China, the Contract Law, and other relevant laws and regulations and judicial interpretations when handling disputes over private lending to safeguard the relation of private lending and protect the legal rights of the parties. However, the Court shall not support and protect any private lending activities involving illegal elements and criminal offences such as gambling, drug abuse or intentional loan to facilitate crimes.

In reality, there are many cases involving illegal loan which are not being protected by law. Some of them even involving criminal liabilities such as illegal fund-raising activities. If the lending activities involve economic crime such as illegal fund-raising, the involved parties are liable to criminal responsibility. It is not strictly simple to differentiate between illegal fund-raising and legal private lending. The crime of illegal fund-raising refers to the act of illegally raising funds from the general public by means of illegal possession as purpose through fraudulent means involving big sum of money via improper channels. The actual crimes in relation to illegal fund-raising include the crime of absorbing public deposits, fund-raising fraud, fraudulent issuance of stocks, bonds and unauthorized issuance of stocks, company bonds and corporate bonds. For serious case involving fraudulent fund-raising, offenders shall be sentenced to fixed-term imprisonment of not more than 10 years or life imprisonment and shall be fined RMB 50,000 to RMB 500,000 or confiscated property. Therefore, companies should pay attention to the legality of their models and channels when raising funds. We would like to give you all a warm reminder that new version of investment such as 'P2P investment' can be risky, investors should be cautious and invest rationally.

Case Sharing: Wu Ying raising fund sentenced to death

In 2012, the Zhejiang Higher People's Court upheld the original verdict and sentenced the 31-year-old offender Wu Ying to death for illegal fund-raising fraud. The case generated many echoes from the society as many people disagreed the death penalty to Wu. Wu had illegally raised fund of RMB 773 million and fraud of illegal fund-raising in the sum of RMB 334 million. Wu Ying was from Zhejiang Dongyang, a legal representative of Zhejiang The True Color Group. She was arrested in the spring of 2007 at her age of 26 and the judgment of First Instance of Jinhua Intermediate People's Court was death penalty.

This case was one of the cases which had great impact on the society in China. Since the first day of the trial, there were voices from the public requesting the abolishment of death penalty for most of the public disagreed that economic crime should be associated with death penalty. In 29 Aug 2015, the 16th Session of the Standing Committee of the 12th National People's Congress voted to pass the Criminal Law Amendment (9), which would be implemented from November 1, 2015 that death penalty was to be abolished for the said type of crime. For now, the maximum penalty for any crime related to illegal fund-raising will be imprisonment for life.

Case Sharing: Hui X Shi Ji Co. Ltd suspected of illegal fraudulent fund-raising involving 30,000 people of RMB 200 million

According to Guangdong Provincial Public Security Department, in late February 2016, the public security department monitored and found that Hui X Shi Ji Co. Ltd P2P online lending platform had restricted the withdrawal of cash and was suspected of illegal fund-raising crimes on the Internet. Potential abnormal problems arose such as the main suspects involving in this crime may be escaped overseas. At the Huanggang custom, the police had accurately captured the main suspect He (Putonghua spelling of a Chinese surname) and immediately captured 3 spots of operation and arrested 400 people on the spot. 19 including the main suspect were arrested and detained after investigation.

- Criminal Law of the People's Republic of China (2017 Amendment）
- Notice of the Supreme People's Court on Legally and Properly Hearing Cases on Disputes over Private Lending to Promote Economic Development and Maintain Social Stability, 2011

Is there a maximum interest rate for lending money to others?

Case Sharing: Loan of 5% per month interest turns to 2% by the Court

As debtor, Miss A borrowed from Mr. BIG EAR in China, stipulated a loan of RMB 500,000 with monthly interest of 5%, the term for the loan was 6 months. On the same day, Mr. BIG EAR transferred RMB 500,000 to Miss A. Yet, Miss A did not return the money as agreed. Mr. BIG EAR sued Miss A for repaying the loan. The court ruled that Miss A shall pay the loan to Mr. BIG EAR in the sum of RMB 500,000 with monthly interest of 2% instead of 5%. Why?

According to the Provisions of the Supreme People's Court on Several Issues Concerning the Application of Law in the Trial of Private Lending Cases, there are two 'lines' and three 'zones' in governing the private lending cases.

- Any interest rate agreed between the debtor and the creditor not exceeding 24% per annum is supported and protected by the Court.
- For interested rate agreed between the debtor and the creditor exceeding 36%, the Court shall rule that the exceeding part (over 36%) will fall into the 'invalid zone' and the Court will not protect nor support the enforcement of exceeding interest rate.
- If the interest rate agreed between the creditor and debtor was between 24% to 36%, it falls into the 'private lending zone' and is not protected by Court, which means that if the part of interest exceeding 24% is cleared, the debtor cannot ask for a return for the exceeding interest, but at the same time, if the exceeding part of the interest is not paid by debtor, the creditor cannot request the debtor to pay the exceeding part.

Case Sharing: Loan sharks in China designing debt traps disguised as legitimate lending

Many victims of a new form of debt trap designed by loan sharks who lend money at exorbitant interest rates with the aim of taking possession of their targets' residences.

The first identified such a trap in 2016 when a woman in Shanghai reported that she had borrowed RMB 200,000 from a financing company (FC) but was forced to pay RMB 600,000 on the second day after the due date, and later another RMB 70,000 to redeem her note.

But the preliminary investigation revealed signed contracts and bank statements, which later determined to be forgeries, indicating that the victim had received RMB 600,000 from FC, which made the case only a civil one.

The case ended up being taken to the court and had the victim's property frozen because of the 'solid evidence' provided by the company FC. The evidence provided by the company's attorney was later on proved forged.

The fraudulent loan scheme looked legitimate, as some criminal gangs even hired professional attorneys, and the scheme was designed to bankrupt the borrowers, who had to repay loans as small as 50,000 yuan with an apartment worth millions of dollar.

Shanghai police then began to crack down on such loan schemes, which target juveniles in most cases. As per report, the city had so far nailed 316 criminal gangs, detained more than 1,770 suspects and retrieved more than RMB 1.2 billion in losses for the victims.

- Reply of the Supreme People's Court regarding the Suggestions on Revising the Provisions on Loan Interest Rate as Prescribed in the Provisions of the Supreme People's Court on Several Issues concerning the Application of Law in Hearing Private Lending Cases, 2019
- Provisions of the Supreme People's Court on Several Issues

concerning the Application of Law in the Trial of Private Lending Cases, 2015

I know that driving after drinking in China is illegal. What is the difference between 'drink driving' and 'drunk driving'?

Drunk driving is a criminal offence in most part of the world. For example, in Hong Kong, drunk driving will cost you a maximum fine of HK$25,000, up to 3 years' imprisonment and 10 driving-offence points. You will also be disqualified from driving for six months to five years.

There are different definitions of drink driving and drunk driving in different places. In China, the definition of drunk driving China is based on the 'Quality Threshold and Inspection of Blood and Expiratory Alcohol Content of Vehicle Drivers' issued by the National Quality Supervision, Inspection and Quarantine Bureau (GB19522:2004). The prescribed limit of drink driving is set at: equal to or more than 20 milligrams and less than 80 milligrams of alcohol per 100ml of blood. Any driver found exceeding the prescribed limit of over 80 milligrams of alcohol per 100ml of blood may face prosecution under the law for drunk driving.

According to regulation related to road traffic safety, drivers with blood alcohol concentrations above 80 milligrams per 100 milliliters are defined as drunk can be convicted of the crime of dangerous driving, despite any circumstances and consequences. The offence will cost the driver a fine and detention. Defendants accused of drunk driving will be exempt from conviction or criminal punishment only if the circumstances are 'obviously minor' or 'minor' in legal term.

Case Sharing: Chen left the scene after drunk drive, insurance company refused to pay

In September 2012, Chen driving the Zhejiang E77××× small vehicle along the Mingzhu Road of Changxing County heading from north to the south, passing the 50-meter section on the south side of Mingzhu Road, driving the electric motor in the same direction as Liu driving an electric motor in the motorway. The two collided, causing damage to the vehicle and a road accident in which Liu was injured. Chen drove away from the scene after an accident and was later arrested by the police for investigation. Liu was injured and was rescued by the hospital and was deceased after a week. After investigation, it was found that Chen was drunk, and his dangerous driving was the major cause of the incident. Finally, Chen was being investigated for his criminal liability and the claims for the damages from insurance compensation was being rejected.

According to law, driver driving a vehicle after alcohol consumption, the driving license of the driver will be detained for up to six months and a fine of over RMB 1,000 and under RMB 2,000 will be imposed. Drink drivers of two attempts will be detained for not more than 10 days and a fine of over RMB 1,000 and under RMB 2,000 will be imposed with driving license being terminated.

- Road Traffic Safety Law of the People's Republic of China (2011 Amendment)
- Opinions of the Supreme People's Court, the Supreme People's Procuratorate and the Ministry of Public Security on Several Issues concerning the Application of Law in the Handling of Criminal Cases of Driving a Motor Vehicle while Intoxicated, 2013

Arrest for illegal posting on internet is heard from time to time, what kind of posting will lead to criminal prosecution?

The freedom of speech in western world is generally higher and sometimes resulted in spreading negative content deliberately. In fact, the standard in allowing messages posted on web differs from one place to another. In 2013, according to the Interpretation of the Supreme People's Court and the Supreme People's Procuratorate on Several Issues Concerning the Application of the Law on the Implementation of the Criminal Law in the Use of Information Networks, the frequency of clicks made to a single message posted on the internet has become a concern. A fabricating fact which damage the reputation of others, being spread (view) over 5,000 times or being shared (repost) by others for over 500 times are considered to be serious offence and reaching the level for prosecution. Therefore, we strong advise everyone to be cautious about your message sharing on social media and blog such as Weibo, the moments of Wechat. Please make sure the content that you share, or follow are valid facts, avoiding falling into traps.

According to law, anyone who publicly insults others or spreads fabricated facts of others by violence or other means reaching the level of serious offence shall be sentenced to fixed-term imprisonment of not more than three years, criminal detention, control or deprivation of political rights. The crime shall be dealt with if it will seriously endanger social order and national interests.

Even in less serious situation, according to law, a person who commits one of the following acts shall be detained for not less than 5 days but not more than 10 days and may, in addition, shall be fined not more than RMB 500; and if the circumstances are relatively minor, he shall be detained for not more than 5 days or be fined not more than RMB 500:

- Intentionally disturbing public order by spreading rumors, making false reports of dangerous situations and epidemic situations or raising false alarms or by other means;
- Disturbing public order by putting in fake hazardous substances such as explosive, toxic, radioactive and corrosive substances or pathogens of infectious diseases; or
- Disturbing public order by threatening to set fire, set off explosions, or put in hazardous substances.

- Interpretation of the Supreme People's Court and the Supreme People's Procuratorate on Several Issues concerning the Specific Application of Law in the Handling of Defamation through Information Networks and Other Criminal Cases, 2013
- Eight Model Cases regarding Infringement upon Personal Rights and Interests by Using the Information Network as Published by the Supreme People's Court, 2014
- Public Security Administration Punishments Law of the People's Republic of China (2012 Amendment)
- Criminal Law of the People's Republic of China (2017 Amendment)

Is prostitution illegal in China?

Prostitution does not violate the Criminal Law of People's Republic of China. But still, prostitution will be considered as violation to the Administration of Public Security. Even though violation of regulations on Penalties for Administration of Public Security is not a criminal offence and does not constitute a crime in criminal law, the offender will be punished according to the Public security management punishment and shall be detained for 15 days in accordance with the Law.

Case Sharing: Famous Actor penalized because of prostitution

In 2014, Police in Beijing has arrested artist Huang in Grand Gongda XX Hotel Beijing on the spot according to report. After investigation, actor Huang admits to prostitution and was sent to a detention facility for detention for 15 days. After that, Beijing police confirmed to the media that Huang Haibo was transferred to shelter education (a type of detained education system under Chinese rules but not the same as imprisonment and is about to discontinue) for another six months because of prostitution. Apart from that, brands with Huang as spokesperson expressed their concern and consideration in terminating the contract with Huang with further action in claiming for compensation from Huang.

According to law, anyone who induces, shelters, introduces any other person to prostitute shall be detained for not less than 10 days but not more than 15 days, and may be concurrently fined RMB 5, 000. If the circumstances are relatively lenient, one will be detained for not more than 5 days or shall be fined not RMB 500. And anyone who produces, transports, copies, sells or rents any obscene book and periodical, picture, film, audio and visual product, etc. or transmitting any obscene information through the computer network, telephone or other telecommunication tools shall be detained for not less than 10 days but not more than 15 days and may be concurrently fined RMB 3, 000. If the circumstances are relatively lenient, one will be detained for not more than 5 days or shall be fined not more than RMB 500.

■ Public Security Administration Punishments Law of the People's Republic of China (2012 Amendment)

If I earn small amount of cash in China, can I bring them along with me when I return to my own country?

China implements a quota management system for currency entry and exit. Chinese citizens entering and leaving the country and foreigners entering and leaving the country must not exceed the limit per person. The specific limits are set by the People's Bank of China. According to regulation related to foreign exchange, anyone who enter sand exits the customs of China shall comply with the restrictions in cash that one can bring along. The restrictions are as follow:

● The customs may allow exiting travelers passing through

customs with cash equivalent to USD 5,000
- For cash equivalent to the amount of USD 5,000 to USD 10,000, travelers need to apply for Permit (available from the withdrawing bank) prior to exiting China. For over USD10,000, shall apply permit from office of Administration of Foreign Exchange by provide relevant supporting document.
- For travelers enter and exit China a several times per day, the limit for foreign currency in cash is USD 500 or below (or any other currency equivalent to the same amount). If any cash or foreign currency is brought along in the amount over USD 500, customs has the right to restrict the exit of the multiple-entries traveler.
- For travelers enter and exit China frequently in a short period of time with 2 exits in 15 days, the limit for bringing cash is USD 1,000. If any cash over USD 1,000, customs has the right to restrict his exit.
- Written approval shall be obtained from the customs for bringing cash over USD 5,000 entering China. For travelers with cash exceed the restricted amount of the customs, the cash will be retained at the customs and sometimes with punishment. After the procedure is completed, the cash will be returned to the traveler.

Case Sharing: Parallel goods smuggling at Hong Kong - Shenzhen borders

In 2014, a 'Gen Y' parallel goods smuggler had been crossing the border at up to 8 times a day. Such case involved two major groups of people, one being the 'smuggler group' and the other the 'owner group'. The owner group was composed of three male adults of the Tsang's brothers, of which two of them were Hongkongers. The brothers had set up trading company in Hong Kong and manufacturing factory in China to deceive their smuggling activities in Taiwan and Hong Kong. The goods involved in the smuggling were Flash Memory, Chipset and SIM card. The owners supply the goods to the 'smuggler group' composed by two members who are Hongkongers (Yu and Cheng) in Hong Kong. The smuggler hided the goods either in their body or inside the luggage and passed through the customs in Lo Wu, Huanggang, Futian. According to the smuggler, each smuggler usually smuggles 2 to 4 times a day for earning a fee of USD 30 each time they pass through the custom. The customs in Shenzhen investigated the records of the smugglers and found that some of the smugglers will go through the customs 8 times a day.

In another case, the customs in Shenzhen caught 10 smugglers, of which 4 of them are Hongkongers and the goods involved were RMB 100 million.

Case Sharing: 10 years of imprisonment for Hongkonger smuggled with tax evasion

In 2013, a Hongkonger Yiu carried 7 bottles of chemical products without declaration to the customs entering Lo Wu. When Yiu exchanged the goods with Zhang at Lo Wu, Yiu was arrested on the spot by the Lo Wu custom officer and confirmed the chemical products as Diamminedichloro palladium (trans-Diamminedichloro palladium(II)). After investigation, Zhang and Yiu had smuggled the chemical products to China during 2013 and assisted in tax evasion activity for over RMB 0.74 million. The Shenzhen People's Procuratorate initiated the public prosecution against Yiu and Zhang. The case was heard at Shenzhen Intermediate People's Court for First Instance Judgement for smuggling of ordinary goods,

Zhang was convicted and sentenced to fixed-term imprisonment of 11 years and be given a pecuniary fine of RMB 500,000 while Yiu was convicted and sentenced to fixed-term imprisonment of 10 years and was given a pecuniary fine of RMB 250,000.

- Exit and Entry Administration of the People's Republic of China, 2012
- Regulations of the People's Republic of China on the Administration of Renminbi, 2018
- Customs Law of the People's Republic of China (2017Amendment)

What expatriates should pay attention to when they are suspected of criminal offences in China?

A typical criminal case will go through three stages, namely, the investigation stage (public security authorities), the review and prosecution stage (People's Procuratorate) and the trial stage (People's Court). According to the Criminal Procedure Law, a criminal suspect has the right to appoint a lawyer as a defender since the first interview or interrogation by the investigating agency or the adoption of compulsory measures (such as detention). Defense lawyers can provide legal assistance to criminal suspects during investigations; proxy complaints and accusations; apply for change of compulsory measures; and collect information related to the suspected crimes and cases, and protect the lawful rights and interests of the parties.

The investigation stage of criminal cases is conducted by the police, who at this time detain suspects, direct interrogations, gather evidence, and interview witnesses. During the investigation stage lawyers' access to case file information is limited, but Criminal Procedure Law states that lawyers are entitled to provide their clients with legal consultation, lodge petitions and complaints, and apply for bail on their clients' behalf. After the investigation stage has been completed, the prosecution procedure begins. At this time, the investigators submit to the People's Procuratorate the evidence that they have gathered for the People's Procuratorate to decide whether the circumstances of the crime are clear and the evidence reliable. During this stage, the defendant is continually entitled to have a legal counsel. Only lawyers are allowed to visit the suspect and lawyers at this point can access and study the full files of the case.

Therefore, if someone is detained or questioned for suspected crimes, first of all, seek legal advice directly from professional lawyers, avoid entrusting any unlicensed intermediaries to handle related matters, and do not believe that someone tells you that 'he knows someone in personal relation who can help with money.' Beware to avoid falling into traps.

- Criminal Procedure Law of the People's Republic of China (2018 Amendment)
- Criminal Law of the People's Republic of China (2017 Amendment)

When I was suspected of criminal offence, shall I remain silence?

In many countries, the person accused or suspected of committing a crime (the suspect) can enjoy the right to remain silent and nemo tenetur seipsum accusare. Nemo tenetur seipsum accusare is a legal maxim in Latin, meaning 'no one is bound to incriminate or accuse himself'. At the moment, the Chinese judicial authorities do not recognize the defendant's right to remain silence. The Criminal Procedure Law states that the criminal suspect shall answer the investigators. At both the pre-trial and trail stage, suspects are expected to answer all questions posed to them in their utmost good faith and to the best of their knowledge. According to law, when interrogating a criminal suspect, the investigating officer shall first examine whether the criminal suspect has committed a criminal act and ask him to state the guilty plot or the innocence and then ask him a question. The suspect shall answer question from the investigator truthfully. However, there is a right to refuse to answer questions that are not related to this case.

Suspect who either confess to their crimes or truthfully report their actions will be rewarded and treated more leniently by the court.

Chinese authorities guarantee the right to retain legal counsel for the suspects. Suspects can hire lawyers to provide legal services for them. Lawyers can meet their clients during interrogations and other forms of investigations such as reviewing, copying, photocopying relevant evidence of the cases. But the law in China does not allow the presence of lawyers during interrogation, in which lawyers cannot be involved in the process of interrogation unless under special circumstances in which there is a language barrier (defendants cannot understand Mandarin). The Ministry of Public Security and People's Procuratorate and the People's Court shall provide translation service to non-Mandarin speaking defendants. In case of forced confession extorted by torture (refers to the use of violence causing physical injuries to the suspect during interrogations), the suspect shall inform the lawyer and initiate charges to be filed and applied for the elimination of false evidence. Forced confession extorted by torture is a criminal offence, it leads to punishment of 3-year fixed term imprisonment or detention.

- Criminal Procedure Law of the People's Republic of China (2018 Amendment)
- Criminal Law of the People's Republic of China (2017 Amendment)

I wish to file a civil litigation in China, what should I pay attention to?

As a plaintiff in civil litigation, one should ensure to identify the subject matter of the disputes is a dispute within the jurisdiction (scope of acceptance) of the Court. Plaintiff should prepare enough evidence as proof and ensure the evidence are authentic, relevant and legal. Before the court proceeding, plaintiff should assign a representative who is clear about the details of the dispute (it can be a lawyer representative or one of the staff within the company). It is wiser for the plaintiff to have everything in written format (according to when, what, how and where in chronological order) supported by evidence and pass to lawyer for analysis and follow up. After the plaintiff confirmed to proceed with the case, as foreign-related case may involve more than one jurisdictions and the choice of law which govern the case matters in deciding the result of the case, the plaintiff should discuss with lawyer and choose the favorable jurisdiction to start the litigation process. Last but not least, the claim must be written properly. In most of the litigation, one of the key elements is the written statement of claim (pleading) of the case which can affect the nature of the case and hence the judgement. The Court in China is even more serious about written evidence and the authentication of the original documents as to compare with courts in the western world.

The parties can choose the law applicable to foreign-related civil relations in accordance with the law. Foreign laws applicable to foreign-related civil relations shall be ascertained by the people's courts, arbitration institutions or administrative organs. Where the parties choose to apply foreign laws, they shall provide the laws of that country.

Other factors that should be paid attention to include the analysis for the legal ground of the dispute, terms and conditions of relevant contract, the jurisdictions and restrictions of the foreign-related contract, the law applicable, the period of prescription (statute of limitations) as well as the fees involved in different stages, the application procedures for the judicial proceedings, etc. To safeguard your rights and interest are being fairly protected and ensure a smooth litigation process, please consult your lawyer for legal advice before initiating a civil procedure.

Case Sharing: Chinese Court Protects Foreigners' IP Equally

China has become increasingly innovative and has demonstrated a serious resolve to enforce an effective Intellectual property rights(IPR) regime. Indeed, as Chinese firms focus on global expansion abroad and high-tech innovation at home, they have increasingly demanded effective IP protections from the government. Many of the concerns raised by foreign companies operating in China have been addressed by legal reforms and new enforcement mechanisms.

China had taken essential measures to protect intellectual property rights and ensure the impartial hearing of IPR cases. For example, in 2014 China established IPR courts in Beijing, Shanghai and Guangzhou. As of June 2017, the courts were collectively accepted 46,000 IPR cases and concluded 33,000 of them. In 2017, IPR tribunals were established in Nanjing, Chengdu, Ningbo, Wuhan, etc. Not only are Chinese companies protected, but foreign companies were protected as well. In 2017, three Chinese shoe factories were fined RMB 10 million by Suzhou Intermediate People's Court for infringing the trademark right of America's New Balance. This was the highest sum of trademark infringement compensation ever gained by foreign parties at that time.

- General Provisions of the Civil Law of the People's Republic of China, 2017
- The Civil Procedure Law of the People's Republic of China (2017 Revision)
- Law of the People's Republic of China on Choice of Law for Foreign-related Civil Relationships, 2010

I have already won a final judgment in a foreign court against the defendant who has a property in China. Can I take a judgment of foreign jurisdiction to enforce it in China?

China is a member of the New York Convention countries and has arrangements with foreign countries for mutual enforcement of arbitral awards. If your commercial disputes have already been decided via legitimate and proper arbitration process in foreign countries and meet the relevant conditions, you can arrange to apply for recognition and enforcement in the Chinese court without filing a lawsuit again in China.

However, if it is a court decision, it is necessary to consider whether there is a mutual recognition of the court judgment.

Up to 2016, China has entered into 37 bilateral judicial assistance treaties on civil or commercial matters, 33 of which contain regulations regarding recognition and enforcement of foreign judgments, namely treaties with Uzbekistan, Kazakhstan, Kirghizia, Tajikistan, Turkey, Cyprus, Laos, Vietnam, Mongolia, Bulgaria, Belarus, Poland, Russia, Romania, Ukraine, Hungary, Lithuania, Spain, Italy, France, Greece, Cuba, Egypt, Morocco, North Korea, United Arab Emirates, Kuwait, Brazil, Argentina, Peru, Algeria, Bosnia and Herzegovina and Tunisia. Decisions rendered by the courts of the above-mentioned states may be enforceable in China.

The limitation period for applying for enforcement of judgments is two years, and the sources of Chinese law regarding enforcement of foreign judgments consist of treaties to which China is a party, legislations, interpretations of laws and case law.

Case Sharing: Recognition and enforcement of a Singapore judgment

The case Kolmar Group AG Co, Ltd v. Jiangsu Textile Import and Export Co, Ltd was an example to demonstrate the Chinese court's attitude toward reciprocity. In this case, the applicant, Kolmar Group AG Co Ltd ('the Kolmar Group'), applied for recognition and enforcement of a civil judgment made by the Singapore High Court. The Nanjing Intermediate People's Court accepted the case, and in the judgment, the court highlighted the basic principles related to recognition and enforcement of a foreign judgement:

- Where an application or request for recognition and enforcement of a legally effective judgment or ruling, the people's court shall examine the application or request in accordance with international treaties concluded or acceded to by the PRC or with the principle of reciprocity.
- If the application or request does not violate the fundamental principles of the laws of the PRC, or State sovereignty, security and social public interests of the PRC, the People's Court shall recognize and enforce the foreign judgment or ruling.
- If the application or request violates the fundamental principles of the law of the PRC or State sovereignty, security and social public interests of the PRC, the People's Court shall not recognize and enforce the foreign judgment or ruling.

In this case, the civil judgment was made by the court of Singapore, and no international treaty has been concluded or jointly acceded to by China and Singapore in the field of mutual recognition and enforcement of a legally effective judgment. However, due to the fact that, in January 2014, the Singapore High Court enforced a civil judgment rendered by the Suzhou Intermediate People's Court, based on the principle of reciprocity, a Chinese court may recognize and enforce the eligible civil judgment issued by a Singapore court. After the examination by this court, the judgment concerned does not contradict with the fundamental principles of Chinese law or violate State sovereignty, security and social public interests of China. The court hence decided to recognize and enforce judgment issued by the Singapore High Court.

This case is in fact one of the rare cases in China that foreign judgments are recognized and enforced based on the principle of reciprocity. If one does not meet the conditions for direct recognition and enforcement, one can entrust a Chinese lawyer to claim against the defendant's property by initiating a new civil case locally.

- The Civil Procedure Law of the People's Republic of China (2017 Revision)
- Reply of the Supreme People's Court to the Request for Instructions on the Application of Siemens International Trading (Shanghai) Co. Ltd. for Recognition and Enforcement of a Foreign Arbitral Award, 2015
- Reply of the Supreme People's Court to the Request of the Higher People's Court of Shandong Province for Instructions on the Case of the Application of Applicant TOYOSHIMA&CO., LTD. and Respondent Gaomi Luyuan Textile Co., Ltd. for the Recognition and Enforcement of A Foreign Arbitral Award, 2015

My Chinese Enterprise believes that an administrative action made by the local government is unreasonable and may harm the interests of enterprise. What can I do?

In China, the Administrative Reconsideration Law and Administrative Litigation Law enacted for the purpose of preventing and correcting any illegal or improper specific administrative acts, protecting the lawful rights and interests of citizens, legal entities and organizations, safeguarding and supervising the exercise of functions and powers by administrative organs in accordance with law. If the specific administrative actions of the government infringe upon the legitimate rights and interests of your enterprise, the enterprise may file an administrative reconsideration with the government or file an administrative lawsuit with the People's Court.

According to law, the people's courts shall protect the right of a citizen, a legal person, or any other organization to file a complaint. And the people court shall accept administrative cases in relation to these kinds of complaints.

Administrative agencies and the employees thereof may not interfere with or impede the acceptance of administrative cases by the people's courts.

Case Sharing: Fireworks Company in Aunhui sued the provincial government won

On December 27, 2013, the Anhui Provincial People's Government Office issued to the Anhui Provincial Safety Supervision Bureau and other departments to inform the 'general exit opinions of fireworks and firecrackers. As such, many fireworks industry enterprise owners who are in debts was bankrupted overnight. After that, many of the firework companies were closed or demolished. The company owners filed a case against the policy through administrative reconsideration and administrative litigation procedure.

On April 20, 2015, the Hefei Intermediate People's Court of Anhui Province made a first-instance judgment, confirming that the administrative action made by the Anhui Provincial People's Government for the overall withdrawal of fireworks and firecrackers was illegal, and requested the provincial government to take corresponding remedial measures within 60 days after the judgment came into effect.

- Administrative Reconsideration Law of the People's Republic of China (2017 Amendment)
- The Administrative Litigation Law of the People's Republic of China (2017 Revision)

I was served as defendant in a civil case for no reason, can I ignore him?

Once you had received a notice from the court that was served to you, you had become the defendant / respondent of the case. At that point, you must be aware that you need to investigate the content of the disputes as shown on the notice including a comprehensive review on the evidence given by the plaintiff. You are reminded not to ignore the case or keep silent even though defendants / respondents have the right choose not the reply in civil cases. Trial in absentia (absence in a trial) is highly not recommended because it means that the defendant / respondent will have no control over the case, allowing the plaintiff / claimant to accuse without boundaries or limitations.

According to law, in civil cases, if the defendant is summoned by subpoena and refuses to appear in court without justified reasons, or if he / she withdraws from the court without the permission of the court, the judgment will be made upon his absence.

In practice, the court's judgment is often unfavorable for the absentee, so it is recommended that the defendant / respondent should be cautious and active in participating in litigation even if one thinks the accusation is completely irrelevant and invalid.

- The Civil Procedure Law of the People's Republic of China (2017 Revision)

If an expatriate has not broken the law, why is he prohibited from leaving China?

China is developing a comprehensive Social Credit System, which is a national reputation system being developed by the Chinese government intended to keep record of citizens and legal entities' creditability, or 'Social Credit'. Authorities can take certain punishing action against a person on the blacklist such as flight ban, exclusion from private schools, exclusion from high prestige work, exclusion from hotels, custom-control and registration on a public blacklist. The social credit system aims to incentivize trustworthy behavior through penalties as well as rewards.

Case Sharing: China bans people from buying travel tickets as part of 'social credit' system

According to news report, discredited travelers were blocked from buying plane or train tickets. Refers to the National Public Credit Information Centre, Chinese courts banned millions would-be travelers from buying flights by the end of 2018. Citizens placed on blacklists for social credit offences were also prevented from buying train tickets. Social credit offences range from not paying individual taxes or fines to spreading false information and taking drugs. According to the report, other penalties for individuals may include being barred from buying insurance, real estate or investment products. Companies on the blacklist are banned from bidding on projects or issuing corporate bonds.

At the moment, the People's Court of China, apart from criminal offences, also holds the power to forbid the involved parties of civil cases to enter and exit China, such measure is named as 'biankong' (custom-control, an initiative to forbid a person from entering and exiting China through control over Immigration procedure) If your debtor travels frequently in and out China, you are suggested to appoint a lawyer to apply to the Court for 'biankong' for your debtor in accordance with legal procedures until settlement has been reached or all the debts are cleared.

Case Sharing: Mediation agreement reached upon a car accident, Hong Kong guy was banned from entering and exiting China for not paying the agreed compensation

In May 2006, a HongKonger Mr. Yip collided with Ms. Zhao from Mainland at a junction of a village in Beijing. Mr. Yip and Ms. Zhao had then reached an agreement in terms of compensation via mediation. Mr. Yip subsequently refused to pay and then Ms. Zhao applied to the court for enforcement. The Courts failed to locate Mr. Yip's whereabouts and failed to inform Mr. Yip, the Court thus filed an order with custom to stop Mr. Yip from entering and exiting China. After being blocked for exit at the border, Mr. Yip then called Ms. Zhao and the Court for settlement by paying the compensation in installments. Mr. Yip paid Ms. Zhao RMB 30,000 upfront and RMB 20,000 per month thereafter until the compensation has completely settled.

According to law, under any of the following circumstances, one shall be prohibited from exiting China, if he:

- does not hold any valid exit-entry credentials or refuses or

evades border inspection;
- has not finished serving a criminal sentence or is the accused or a suspect in a criminal case;
- is prohibited from exiting China as decided by a people's court for involvement in a pending civil case;
- has received a criminal penalty for disrupting national border administration or has been repatriated by any other country or region for illegal exit from China, illegal residence or illegal employment and the prescribed period of prohibition from exiting China has not expired;
- is prohibited from exiting China as decided by the relevant competent department of the State Council because the national security or interest may be compromised; or
- Other circumstances as set out by laws and administrative regulations under which the Chinese citizen is prohibited from exiting China.

■ Exit and Entry Administration of the People's Republic of China, 2012

www.ingramcontent.com/pod-product-compliance
Lightning Source LLC
Chambersburg PA
CBHW072135170526
45158CB00004BA/1376